SECOND EDITION

Differentiated Instructional Strategies

OTHER CORWIN PRESS BOOKS BY
GAYLE H. GREGORY & CAROLYN CHAPMAN

Teacher Teams That Get Results:
61 Group Process Skills and Strategies
by Gayle H. Gregory and Lin Kuzmich, forthcoming

Differentiated Reading and Writing Strategies for Elementary Classrooms
(A Multimedia Kit for Professional Development)
by Carolyn Chapman and Rita King, forthcoming

Differentiated Reading and Writing Strategies for Middle and High School Classrooms
(A Multimedia Kit for Professional Development)
by Carolyn Chapman and Rita King, forthcoming

Designing Brain Compatible Learning (Third Edition)
by Gayle H. Gregory and Terence Parry, 2006

Differentiating Instruction With Style:
Aligning Teacher and Learner Intelligences for Maximum Achievement
by Gayle H. Gregory, 2005

Differentiated Assessment Strategies:
One Tool Doesn't Fit All
by Carolyn Chapman and Rita King, 2004

Differentiated Literacy Strategies for Student Growth and Achievement in Grades 7–12
by Gayle H. Gregory and Lin Kuzmich, 2005

Differentiated Literacy Strategies for Student Growth and Achievement in Grades K–6
by Gayle H. Gregory and Lin Kuzmich, 2004

Data Driven Differentiation in the Standards-Based Classroom
by Gayle H. Gregory and Lin Kuzmich, 2004

Differentiated Instructional Strategies for Reading in the Content Areas
by Carolyn Chapman and Rita King, 2003

Differentiated Instructional Strategies for Writing in the Content Areas
by Carolyn Chapman and Rita King, 2003

Differentiated Instructional Strategies in Practice:
Training, Implementation, and Supervision
by Gayle H. Gregory, 2003

SECOND EDITION

Differentiated Instructional Strategies

One Size Doesn't Fit All

Gayle H. Gregory · Carolyn Chapman

CORWIN PRESS
A SAGE Publications Company
Thousand Oaks, California

For information:

Corwin Press
A Sage Publications Company
2455 Teller Road
Thousand Oaks, California 91320
www.corwinpress.com

Sage Publications Ltd.
1 Oliver's Yard
55 City Road
London EC1Y 1SP
United Kingdom

Sage Publications India Pvt. Ltd.
B-42, Panchsheel Enclave
Post Box 4109
New Delhi 110 017 India

Printed in the United States of America

Library of Congress Cataloging-in-Publication Data

Gregory, Gayle.
Differentiated instructional strategies : one size doesn't fit all / Gayle H. Gregory, Carolyn Chapman.—2nd ed.
    p. cm.
Includes bibliographical references and index.
ISBN 1-4129-3639-X or 978-1-4129-3639-2 (cloth)—ISBN 1-4129-3640-3 or 978-1-4129-3640-8 (pbk.)
    1. Individualized instruction. 2. Cognitive styles in children. 3. Mixed ability grouping in education. I. Chapman, Carolyn. II. Title.
LB1031.G74 2007
371.39′4—dc22   2006019606

This book is printed on acid-free paper.

06 07 08 09 10   10 9 8 7 6 5 4 3 2 1

Acquisitions Editor:	Faye Zucker
Editorial Assistant:	Gem Rabanera
Production Editor:	Laureen A. Shea
Copy Editor:	Carla Freeman
Typesetter:	C&M Digitals (P) Ltd.
Proofreaders:	Theresa Kay and Dennis Webb
Indexer:	Nara Wood
Cover Designer:	Rose Storey
Graphic Designer:	Lisa Miller

Illustrations by Tammy Kay Brunson, Thomson, GA 30824

CONTENTS

learning-styles theories, identifies multiple intelligences, and provides tools to help teachers identify their students' learning styles and preferences.

4. Assessing the Learner — 47

Everyone needs feedback. Teachers and students need to exchange constant feedback to monitor progress and to adjust learning. It has been said that assessment drives the curriculum. Teachers need pre-assessment tools to plan for learning as well as ongoing assessment tools to use during and after the learning process. Pre-assessment is essential for teachers to find out what students know, can do, and are interested in learning. If teachers use pre-assessment data when they are planning lessons, learners are not bored by repeating "history" or, conversely, lost with no frame of reference when the new learning is beyond their realm of experience. Suggestions and examples of effective pre-assessment tools are outlined as well as tools to use during and after the learning process. Ideas for grading are explored.

5. Adjusting, Compacting, and Grouping — 71

After pre-assessment, teachers need to examine the data and adjust the learning based on students' knowledge, skills, past experiences, preferences, and needs. A practical process is shared that allows teachers to adjust learning. With knowledgeable and capable learners, compacting is a strategy that sometimes can be used, and several ways of compacting are shared and explained. Processes for grouping students for a variety of reasons are explored, and techniques to form groups and design interactions are examined. The chapter works with the acronym TAPS, representing Total or whole group, Alone or independent, Partner work, or Small-group interaction.

6. Instructional Strategies for Student Success   95

Teachers everywhere are paying attention to how the brain works and makes meaning, and to what should go on in classrooms as a result of that knowledge. An instructional repertoire is a necessary component of classrooms that have a greater capacity to reach all learners. If students do not understand content (or process or concept) the first time the teacher presents it, "saying it louder and slower in another part of the room" will not make it any clearer. Extensive research is now available on best practices and pedagogy that make a difference in student achievement. This research is explored, and brain-based strategies are outlined.

7. Curriculum Approaches for Differentiated Classrooms   133

There are a variety of useful curriculum approaches for facilitating differentiated learning. This chapter explains Centers, Projects, Choice Boards, Problem-Based Learning, Inquiry Models, and Contracts and provides examples for each approach.

8. Putting It All Together in Your Differentiated Classroom

Coming full circle in this chapter, we revisit the lesson-planning template introduced in Chapter 1 and the adjustable-assignments grid from Chapter 5. This chapter applies the template and the grid to a variety of differentiated lessons at various levels—early, elementary, middle, and high school—and also uses them to differentiate by content, interest, readiness, and multiple intelligences for the diverse learners in your classroom.

PREFACE

TWO EXPERIENCED EDUCATORS DEVELOPED THIS BOOK: Gayle Gregory and Carolyn Chapman, both consultants, trainers, and authors. It responds to educators who have seen a need for an organized, practical, and comprehensive way to plan for classroom instruction that meets the needs of diverse learners in heterogeneous classrooms.

We are indebted to other professional educators for their work, writings, and examples and to family members for their love and support.

To our husbands, Joe and Jim, we express our thanks for understanding and encouragement in the long hours of writing, for ideas, listening, and editing.

We have been influenced and enlightened by outstanding professionals, such as Pat Wolfe, Howard Gardner, Daniel Goleman, David Sousa, Bob Sylwester, Eric Jensen, Tony Gregorc, Bernice McCarthy, Carol Rolheiser, Bob Marzano, Jay McTighe, Carol Ann Tomlinson, Carol O'Connor, Pam Robbins, Rita King, Robin Fogarty, and Kay Burke, to mention a few.

We would also like to thank the teachers who allowed us to borrow sample lessons from them for this volume: Diane Huggler, Ellen Wilken, Cindy Palur, Jamie Downhower, Drew Tessler, Keisha Gabriel, Sarward Baig and Linda Smeutek, Ana Solis, and Michael Bait.

Special thanks go to friends and colleagues Joanne Quinn and Rita King, whose ongoing enthusiasm and support and good questions have helped clarify many issues in this book.

We dedicate this book to children everywhere in the hope that its content will help teachers meet their needs and empower learners to reach their potential and be the best they can be with joy, enthusiasm, creativity, and self-confidence.

Corwin Press gratefully acknowledges the contributions of the following reviewers:

Maria Elena Reyes, Assistant Professor, School of Education, University of Alaska Fairbanks, AK

Kathleen Chamberlain, Assistant Professor of Education, Lycoming College, Williamsport, PA

Sarah Rees Edwards, Adjunct Professor, University of Arizona, Tucson, AZ

Gayle H. Gregory has been a teacher in elementary, middle, and secondary schools. For many years, she taught in schools with extended periods of instructional time (block schedules). She has had extensive districtwide experience as a curriculum consultant and staff development coordinator. She was course director at York University for the Faculty of Education, teaching in the teacher education program. She now consults internationally (Europe, Asia, North and South America, Australia) with teachers, administrators, and staff developers in the areas of brain-compatible learning, block scheduling, emotional intelligence, instructional and assessment practices, cooperative group learning, presentation skills, renewal of secondary schools, enhancing teacher quality, coaching and mentoring, and managing change. She is affiliated with many organizations, including the Association for Supervision and Curriculum Development and the National Staff Development Council. In addition to her many books on differentiated instructional strategies, she also is the coauthor of *Teacher Teams That Get Results*, *Designing Brain-Compatible Learning*, and *Thinking Inside the Block Schedule: Strategies for Teaching in Extended Periods of Time*. She has been featured in *Video Journal of Education*'s editions on "Differentiated Instruction." She is committed to lifelong learning and professional growth for herself and others. She may be contacted by calling (905) 336-6565 or by e-mail at gregorygayle@netscape.net. Her Web site is http://www3.sympatico.ca/gayle.gregory.

Carolyn Chapman continues her life's goal as an international educational consultant, author, and teacher. She supports educators in their process of change for today's students. She has taught in a variety of settings, from kindergarten to college classrooms. Her interactive, hands-on, professional development opportunities focus on challenging the mind to ensure success for learners of all ages. In her books and her professional development opportunities, participants are engaged in exciting active learning that puts theory into practice. She walks her walk and talks her talk to make a difference in the journey of learning in today's classrooms. Carolyn and her husband, Jim, currently run the company she founded, Creative Learning Connection, Inc.

She has authored and coauthored a number of books. In addition to her writing experience, she has been featured in several multimedia resources on differentiated instruction by *Video Journal of Education* and by Corwin Press. Her book publications include *Differentiated Instructional Strategies: One Size Doesn't Fit All, Differentiated Assessment Strategies: One Tool Doesn't Fit All, Test Success in the Brain-Compatible Classroom, Differentiated Instructional Strategies for Reading in the Content Areas, Differentiated Instructional Strategies for Writing in the Content Areas, If the Shoe Fits . . . How to Develop Multiple Intelligences in the Classroom, Multiple Assessments for Multiple Intelligences,* and *Multiple Intelligences Through Centers and Projects.* Her company, Creative Learning Connection, Inc., has produced a CD, *Carolyn Chapman's Making the Shoe Fit,* and published training manuals based on each of her books. Each of these publications demonstrates her desire and determination to make an effective impact for educators and students.

Carolyn may be contacted through the Creative Learning Connection, Inc., at (706) 597-0706, e-mail at cchapman@carolynchapman.com, or through her Web site at http://www.carolynchapman.com.

NO ONE WOULD EVER SAY THAT ALL STUDENTS ARE THE SAME. Certainly no teacher or parent would tell you that. Yet in schools, we often treat students as if they were, even though all those faces look so different. We sometimes put them through the same hoops, even though we know it isn't making a difference for all of them. Experience, as well as the research we now have about the human brain, tells us that students are different, that they learn differently and have different likes, preferences, and needs.

We have used the analogy of "One size doesn't fit all" for years in education (see Figure 1). We know that students are different from one another in height, size, shape, hair and eye color, and background and experience. As with clothing, we would not buy or make the same garments for all learners (even school uniforms, although they look the same, are sized and adjusted and accessorized for the wearer) because they would not fit, suit, or be comfortable. Students differ from each other in physical abilities and social development as well.

Figure 1.   As With Clothing, So With Lessons: One Size Does Not Fit All

Yet for years we have planned "The Lesson" and taught it to all, knowing that we were boring some and losing others because they were not ready for that learning. Still, we expect students to adjust to the learning when the learning should really be adjusted to the learner. Adjustments should be based on the sound knowledge of the learner. This includes what they know already, can do, like, are like, need, or prefer.

Effective teachers must know the standards and their students. The standards and the needs of the students should determine instructional decisions. Programs, materials, and resources should not guide curriculum and instruction. The specific materials and resources are selected to teach to the needs of the particular group of students and the standards being taught.

Our quest in schools and classrooms everywhere is to foster success for students in their lives through becoming self-directed, productive problem solvers and thinkers. For years, we have been studying and implementing research-based instructional strategies and assessment tools that make a difference in student achievement. *Differentiation* is a philosophy that enables educators to plan strategically in order to reach the needs of the diverse learners in classrooms today to achieve targeted standards. Differentiation is not a set of tools, but a belief system educators embrace to meet the unique needs of every learner.

Supporters of differentiation as a philosophy believe:

- All students have areas of strength.
- All students have areas that need to be strengthened.
- Each student's brain is as unique as a fingerprint.
- It is never too late to learn.
- When beginning a new topic, students bring their prior knowledge base and experience to the learning.
- Emotions, feelings, and attitudes affect learning.
- All students can learn.
- Students learn in different ways at different times.

By using differentiated strategies and activities, educators are implementing this philosophy daily in classrooms across the grade levels and content areas.

Differentiating instruction is not new, but requires a more conscious effort to analyze available data and make decisions about what is working and what needs to be adjusted. Keep what works. Discard practices that don't work. Change what needs changing. Educators are already doing a great job! More conscious consideration and a greater repertoire of strategies will help educators do an even better job.

THE DIFFERENTIATED CLASSROOM

A *differentiated classroom* is one in which the teacher responds to the unique needs of students. Carol Ann Tomlinson (1999) names content, process, and product as things that are differentiated in a classroom. The content is what is taught. The way a learner interprets, adapts, and finds ownership is the process. The product shows the learner's personal interpretation and what he or she knows. Differentiated instruction gives a variety of options to successfully reach targeted standards. It meets learners where they are and offers challenging, appropriate options for them in order to achieve success.

Teachers can strategically and effectively differentiate

- content
- assessment tools
- performance tasks
- instructional strategies

Differentiating Content

One way to differentiate is to provide different content to meet the varying needs of students. Content teaches the standards and meets the needs of the particular students being taught. The information to teach and the resources to best teach it are selected strategically. This is implemented by

- using different genres
- leveling materials
- using a variety of instructional materials
- providing choice
- using selective abandonment

Differentiating Assessment Tools

Most teachers are already effectively differentiating assessment during and after the learning. However, it is equally important to assess knowledge and interests prior to the learning. Understanding what students know about the upcoming topic is essential to planning quality learning experiences. Dispense a blending of formal and informal tools for ongoing assessment.

Differentiating Performance Tasks

Students demonstrate their knowledge in many different ways. Provide various opportunities and choices for learners to show what they know. For example, students can choose how to demonstrate their knowledge by creating a prop, giving an oral report, or engaging in a center experience.

Differentiating Instructional Strategies

When teachers vary instructional strategies and activities, more students learn content and information and they develop the necessary skills. By targeting diverse intelligences and learning styles, teachers can label learning activities in ways that help students choose when to work with their areas of strength and when to work with areas that still need strengthening. Using research-based best practices (Marzano, Pickering, & Pollack, 2001) will help ensure that more students develop the concepts and skills targeted. Rehearsal in a variety of ways helps learning become part of long-term memory.

As in clothing, "One size doesn't fit all," so in classrooms one way is not the only way.

WHY DIFFERENTIATION?

We have been faced with more change than ever before in education. Several decades ago, teachers came into the profession with a desire to work with children, a knowledge base, and good intentions. Today, teachers face a challenging landscape that is in constant flux. Many factors influence the constantly changing classroom:

- Standard-based classrooms: targeted expectations set by districts, states, and nations
- High expectations for all students: no longer can we leave children behind and just "spray and pray" for success
- Multicultural diversity: continuous influx of immigrant children with little or no communication skills or competencies in English
- Student diversity: unique learning styles and different levels of multiple intelligences
- New cognitive research on human learning: knowledge of the brain and how it processes memory and makes meaning
- Rapid societal and technological change: political and economic revolutions that influence what and how learning takes place

Along with all these changes, schools are expected to put the "C.A.R.T. before the horse." The acronym C.A.R.T. stands for

C onnected, Competence, Confidence, Compassion

A cceptance, Affection, Appreciation

R eading, 'Riting, and 'Rithmetic and also Responsibility, Respect, and Relationships

T hinking, Technology, Teamwork

All these C.A.R.T. skills and attributes are necessary to be successful in life, not just at school. Schools are expected to build in opportunities within the curriculum for students to practice and develop these skills. However, the balancing act is dealing with district and state standards and the reality that classrooms contain a diverse, heterogeneous group of learners. Learners with different cultural backgrounds and different experiences, interests, learning styles, and multiple intelligences are the norm.

Students don't all learn the "same thing in the same way on the same day." As educators in classrooms, we need to consider each child within the learning community, based on his or her needs, readiness, preferences, and interests.

We live and work in a global society of high accountability. The legislative notion that any educator would willingly "leave a child behind" is insulting to most educators who view their chosen profession as a "mission" rather than as a job.

For many decades, educators used a "bell curve" to rank students. They didn't expect everyone to succeed. It was more the norm to "teach, test, and hope for the best."

Today, however, we do expect that all students will learn to their full potential and that all teachers will find a way to enable each individual to be successful. Dr. R. L. Canady, of the University of Virginia, shared that there are three groups of students in classrooms:

- A group of 25% to 37% of students learn "in spite of us." Those are the students who come ready, willing, and prepared to play the school game in order to succeed. These learners see education as a means to an end, do the work as assigned regardless of preferences, and have the support of significant others in their lives.

- A group of 15% to 25% of students are identified as having some exceptionality and receive additional resources.

- A large group of about 37% to 50% learn because of the teacher's skills and efforts and because of appropriate instruction and assessment aligned with targeted standards.

Through differentiation, we give all these students the opportunity to learn to their full potential. Throughout this book, we explore the elements needed in the differentiated classroom to engage students and to facilitate learning to increase the chances that all learners will succeed. Figure 2 organizes these elements in categories listing tools and strategies that build an inclusive, nurturing classroom and allow teachers to design learning to honor the diversity of the learning population.

Figure 2. Tools and Strategies for Designing Inclusive Differentiated Classrooms for Diverse Learners

Climate	Knowing the Learner	Assessing the Learner	Adjustable Assignments	Instructional Strategies	Curriculum Approaches
Safe	**Learning Styles**	**Before**	Compacting	**Brain/Research Based**	Centers
Nurturing	Dunn & Dunn	*Formal*		Memory model	
Encourages	Gregorc	Pretest	TAPS	Elaborative rehearsal	Projects
Risk Taking	Silver/Strong/Hanson	Journaling		Focus activities	
			Total Group	Graphic organizers	Choice Boards
Multisensory	**Multiple Intelligences**	*Informal*	Lecturette	Compare & contrast	
Stimulating	Using observation	Squaring off	Presentation	Webbing	Problem-Based
	checklists, inventories,	Boxing	Demonstration	Metaphorical thinking	Learning
Complex	logs, and journals to	Graffiti facts	Jigsaw	Cooperative group learning	
	become more aware		Video	Jigsaw	Inquiry Models
Challenging	of how students learn	**During**	Field trip	Questioning	
		Formal	Guest speaker	Cubing	Contracts
Collaborative		Journaling/Portfolios	Text	Role-play	
		Teacher-made tests			
Team and Class		Checklists/Rubrics	*Alone*		
Building			Interest		
		Informal	Personalized		
Norms		Thumb it	Multiple intelligences		
		Fist of five			
		Face the fact	*Paired*		
			Random		
		After	Interest		
		Formal	Task		
		Posttest			
		Portfolio/Conferences	*Small Groups*		
		Reflections	Heterogeneous		
			Homogeneous		
		Informal	Task oriented		
		Talking topics	Constructed		
		Conversation	Random		
		Circles	Interest		
		Donut			

PLANNING FOR DIFFERENTIATED INSTRUCTION

A planning model (see Figure 3) can be used to help teachers make decisions about differentiated instruction and assessment. Each phase of the planning model will be explained. Throughout this book, the strategies are clarified using examples.

1. Establish what needs to be taught. First, consider the standards, benchmarks, essential questions, or expectations to be taught. It should be clear what the students should know, be able to do, or be like after the learning experience. Determine which assessment strategies will be used to collect data (logs, checklists, journals, observations, portfolios, rubrics).

   Essential questions may be developed that will be visible and posted throughout the unit so that students can consider the questions as they work on tasks.

2. Identify the content, including facts, vocabulary, and essential skills.

3. Activate. Determine what students know and what they need to learn next. This may be done 1 to 3 weeks prior to the unit to allow plenty of time for planning learning activities, grouping students, and raising anticipation about the new topic. "Emotional hooks" can be used to engage and to capture the attention of the students through challenge, novelty, and unique experiences.

   A strong pre-assessment determines what the students know. The pre-assessment is sometimes formal and other times informal. It is essential to select an assessment tool that best shows students' prior knowledge, background experience, and attitudes and preferences toward the information.

4. Acquire. Decide what new information and skills students need to learn and how they will acquire the knowledge. Also decide whether the acquisition will take place in a total group setting or in small groups.

   Now it is time to lay out the plan. Determine how the information is best taught to this particular group of students. In this step, weed through the resources available and find the materials that will best meet the needs of these students. Focus on quality materials and remember that what works for one group does not always work for another group.

5. Apply and Adjust. Students need the opportunity to practice and become actively engaged with the new learning in order to understand and retain it. Determine how the students will be grouped and what tasks will be assigned to challenge them at the appropriate levels.

6. Assess. Decide how the students will demonstrate their knowledge. Consider providing choices for doing so.

All these decisions are made with the intention of honoring the diversity of the students' learning styles, multiple intelligences, and personal interests.

So, let's get started exploring the facets of differentiating instruction and offering our students diverse opportunities to succeed.

Figure 3. The Six-Step Planning Model for Differentiated Learning: Template		
Planning for Differentiated Learning		
1. STANDARDS: What should students know and be able to do?		Assessment tools for data collection: (logs, checklists, journals, agendas, observations, portfolios, rubrics, contracts)
Essential Questions:		
2. CONTENT: (concepts, vocabulary, facts)	**SKILLS:**	
3. ACTIVATE: Pre-assessment Prior knowledge & engaging the learners	Focus Activity: Pre-assessment strategy	• Quiz, test • Surveys • K-W-L • Journals • Arm gauge • Give me • Brainstorm • Concept formation • Thumb it
4. ACQUIRE: Total group or small groups		• Lecturette • Presentation • Demonstration • Jigsaw • Video • Field trip • Guest speaker • Text
5. Grouping Decisions: (TAPS, random, heterogeneous, homogeneous, interest, task, constructed) **APPLY** **ADJUST**		• Learning centers • Projects • Contracts • Compact/Enrichment • Problem based • Inquiry • Research • Independent study
6. ASSESS Diversity Honored (learning styles, multiple intelligences, personal interest, etc.)		• Quiz, test • Performance • Products • Presentation • Demonstration • Log, journal • Checklist • Portfolio • Rubric • Metacognition

CLASSROOMS EVERYWHERE OFFER A DIVERSITY OF FACES AND shapes and sizes, but underneath the diversity, there are fundamental elements that all learners need in order to succeed and to feel positive about their experiences in school.

WHAT DO LEARNERS NEED TO SUCCEED?

For students to succeed, they need to believe that they can learn and that what they are learning is useful, relevant, and meaningful for them. They need to know that they belong in the classroom and that they are responsible for their own learning and behavior. This develops a self-directed learner who is confident in making the information his or her own. This instills *self-efficacy,* which means believing in oneself. In *Education on the Edge of Possibility,* Caine and Caine (1997) state,

> Teachers' beliefs in and about human potential and in the ability of all children to learn and achieve are critical. These aspects of the teachers' mental models have a profound impact on the learning climate and learner states of mind that teachers create. Teachers need to understand students' feelings and attitudes will be involved and will profoundly influence student learning. (p. 124)

Effective teachers believe that all students can learn and be successful. Effective teachers consciously create a climate in which all students feel included. Effective teachers believe that there is potential in each learner and commit to finding the key that will unlock that potential.

CLASSROOM CULTURE AND LEARNING COMMUNITIES

Culture is often referred to as "the way we do things around here." People who live and work in a culture sometimes can't explain or describe it, but they can certainly sense it. Culture may not necessarily be conveyed only through words, but also through actions. Sometimes what we do screams so loudly that we can't hear what is being said. In the words of DePorter, Reardon, and Singer-Nourie (1998), in their book *Quantum Teaching,* "Everything Speaks, Everything Always." They caution teachers that what they do, say, and allude to have an effect on learners and their perceptions of success. According to Gregory and Parry (2006),

> As far as the brain is concerned, actions speak louder than words. Everything that happens in the classroom is monitored by three parts of the brain, two of which have no spoken language but are very adept at reading body language and tone of voice. Every gesture, every inflection, and every invasion of personal space is monitored by the limbic system and evaluated in terms of its threat potential. These skills allowed our ancestors to survive and they are still alive and well in all of us. (p. 13)

Because the brain is a *parallel processor,* it absorbs information on a conscious and an unconscious level. The brain constantly performs many functions at the same time (Ornstein & Thompson, 1984). It therefore can manage to process thoughts, emotions, and perceptions simultaneously.

The brain is also a parallel processor in that it facilitates learning by involving both focused attention and peripheral perception. O'Keefe and Nadel (1978) state that the brain responds to the entire sensory context in which learning takes place. *Peripheral stimuli* include everything in the classroom, from the drab or colorful walls to subtle clues, such as a look or gesture, that conveys meaning and is interpreted by the brain. All sounds and visual signals are full of complex messages. A sarcastic remark can speak volumes to a sensitive learner, and a gesture can convey far more than the spoken word.

In his work with the Mid-continent Research for Education and Learning (McREL) group and with Dimensions of Learning, Robert Marzano (1992) examined the climate for learning, as did Jay McTighe (1990), with the Maryland State Department of Education:

> Closely related to teachers' behavior is the development of a classroom climate conducive to good thinking . . . students cannot think well in a harsh, threatening situation or even in a subtly intimidating environment where group pressure makes independent thinking unlikely. Teachers can make their classrooms more thoughtful places by demonstrating in their actions that they welcome originality and differences of opinion.

Noted researcher Deborah Rozman (1998) remarked that "the neural information the heart sends to the brain can either facilitate or inhibit cortical function, affecting perception, emotional response, learning, and decision making." The heartbeat of another person is perceivable within 3 to 4 feet, because of the electromagnetic field that it projects. The heartbeat of one person registers in the brainwaves of another person. There are intuitive or gut feelings that are picked up by neurons throughout the body. It has often been said, "People need to know you care before they care what you know." And old adages become just that because they are usually true.

As part of his choice theory of motivation, William Glasser (1990, 1998) cites five equally important needs:

- The need to survive and reproduce
- The need to belong and love
- The need to have some power

- The need to have freedom
- The need to have fun

This is also evident in Abraham Maslow's (1968) well-known hierarchy of needs, which includes the following, beginning with the most basic:

- Physiological needs: food, water, air, shelter
- Safety needs: security, freedom from fear, order
- Belongingness and love: friends, spouse, children
- Self-esteem: self-respect, achievement, reputation
- Self-actualization: becoming what the individual has the potential to become

Human beings generally move up the hierarchy from basic to complex needs. As each need has been met, it becomes less of a motivator as the person focuses on the next level.

As we examine motivators, we need to remember that basic needs have to be met first for students. We recognize that all humans have a very strong need to be liked and included. Classrooms everywhere must foster an inclusionary climate. It is essential that students bond with one another and with the teacher to form a positive learning community. Dr. Robert Sapolsky (1998), professor of biological sciences and neuroscience at Stanford University, states that we can minimize the impact of stress by building a supportive environment:

> Put an infant primate through something unpleasant: it gets a stress-response. Put it through the same stressor while in a room full of other primates and . . . it depends. If those primates are strangers, the stress-response gets worse. But if they are friends, the stress-response is decreased. Social support networks—it helps to have a shoulder to cry on, a hand to hold, an ear to listen to you, someone to cradle you and to tell you it will be okay. (p. 215)

Some teachers with their students cooperatively develop classroom "agreements" (Gibbs, 1995), "Trust Statements" (Harmin, 1994), or "rules to live by" to help students feel that they have a voice in the running of the classroom. These rules also help students become more emotionally intelligent and responsible learners. Students in small groups generate statements that they believe the class should live by, for example, "Everyone's ideas count." After the groups share their statements, the class combines, deletes, or adds sentences until consensus is reached and students feel comfortable and can support these rules to live by, which may include the following:

- There is no wrong opinion.
- No put-downs or sarcasm here.
- Everyone must be heard.
- Mistakes are learning points.

If these statements are posted for all students to see and reflect on, students will monitor and honor the rules that they have created.

We also recognize that learning communities foster links between heart and mind. Driscoll (1994) asks us to consider the following:

> Community is the entity in which individuals derive meaning. It is not so much characterized by shared space as it is by shared meanings. Community in this view is not a mere artifact of people living (or working or studying) in the same place, but is rather a rich source of living tradition. (p. 3)

EMOTIONS AND LEARNING

Students living in fear cannot learn. The phenomenon of "downshifting," "the psychophysiological response to threat associated with fatigue or perceived helplessness" (Caine & Caine, 1997, p. 18), suggests that students will not attend to learning if their major concern is safety. This analogy is helpful in planning, so that we challenge students in ways appropriate to their skill levels without overstressing them. Some students may already be so stressed from difficult situations in their personal lives that they are unable to fully attend to lessons, as they are on "high alert" (Gregory & Parry, 2006).

Safety in classrooms means intellectual safety as well as physical safety. During stress, the emotional centers of the brain take control of cognitive functioning, and thus the rational, thinking part of the brain is not as efficient, and this can cause learning to be impeded. If students are living daily with the threat of being ridiculed or bullied, they cannot give their full attention to learning. Students who are challenged beyond their skill levels are more concerned about being embarrassed or laughed at than with the quest for learning. They will not be motivated to attempt the challenge if they aren't able to imagine or perceive success.

In classrooms where the teacher does not adjust the learning to the students' levels of readiness and teaches only to the "middle," some students will be bored from lack of challenge, and others may be placed under undue stress from too great a challenge. Thus, teachers need to consider where their learners are in relation to the learning goal and plan learning experiences just beyond the skill level of each student.

All students are more likely to be engaged in the learning, rise to the challenge, and have a sense of self-confidence as they approach the task if they feel that they have a chance to succeed. Thus, once the levels of readiness have been considered (although it is unrealistic to consider each learner individually), students can often be grouped and experiences designed to accommodate the learners at their levels of understanding.

Teachers need to consider the degree of complexity of learning tasks so that they will be challenging but not overwhelming. This establishes the state of "flow" (Csikszentmihalyi, 1990), the condition that exists when learners are so engaged, excited about learning, challenged, and receiving appropriate feedback that they are oblivious to anything else. Students are at their most productive and most creative in this state:

> People seem to concentrate best when the demands on them are a bit greater than usual, and they are able to give more than usual. If there is too little demand on them, people are bored. If there is too much for them to handle, they get anxious. Flow

occurs in that delicate zone between boredom and anxiety. (Goleman, 1992, as cited in Csikszentmihalyi, 1990, p. 4)

Renate Caine, a well-known pioneer in the field of brain-based education, proposes that there are three basic elements to brain/mind learning and teaching:

- Emotional climate and relationship or relaxed alertness
- Instruction or immersion in complex experience
- Consolidation of learning or active processing

Emotional climate and relationships are important in producing what Kohn (1993) refers to as "relaxed alertness":

All the methodologies that are used to orchestrate the learning context influence the state of relaxed alertness. It is particularly important for educators to understand the effect of rewards and punishments on student states of mind. Research shows most applications of reward and punishment in the behavioral mode inhibit creativity, interfere with intrinsic motivation, and reduce the likelihood of meaningful learning. (as cited in Caine & Caine, 1997, p. 123)

Rewards and punishments tend to lessen the chances of self-motivation and an appreciation of learning as its own reward. Five practical alternatives to using rewards are the following:

- Eliminating threat
- Creating a strongly positive climate
- Increasing feedback
- Setting goals
- Activating and engaging positive emotions (Jensen, 1998b, p. 68)

It is important, if not imperative, that students feel good, have success, have friends, and celebrate their learning:

Emotions affect student behavior because they create distinct, mind-body states. A state is a moment composed of a specific posture, breathing rate, and chemical balance in the body. The presence or absence of norepinephrine, vasopressin, testosterone, serotonin, progesterone, dopamine, and dozens of other chemicals dramatically alters your frame of mind and body. How important are states to us? They are all that we have; they are our feelings, desires, memories, and motivations. (Jensen, 1998b, p. 75)

The emotional environment interacts with instruction and influences how information is consolidated. If "downshifting" occurs, the high stress/threat response sabotages connections and thus learning cannot take place. At this point, we are fortunate if even memorization of isolated facts and programmed skills is possible. It is almost impossible for higher-order thinking to take place.

If students think that success isn't possible because the task is too difficult or instructions for a task are ambiguous and not understood, they feel uncertain. These situations cause the learner to form a negative state, and the learner ceases to persevere. Alternately, classrooms that create "eustress" or a state of "flow" create a positive learning environment. Classrooms that embed choices in learning and routines that demonstrate mutual respect are supportive learning environments for students.

EMOTIONAL INTELLIGENCE

Emotional intelligence is a person's ability to use his or her emotions intelligently. It involves maintaining a balance between reason and emotion. Daniel Goleman (1995) organizes emotional intelligence as a set of emotional competencies that occur in five domains.

Self-Awareness

Self-awareness is one's ability to sense and name a feeling when it happens and also to put it into words. Self-aware people can use appropriate strategies to deal with their moods by sharing frustrations with others or seeking support on a bad day. Teachers should encourage students to articulate their feelings and seek and give support. Self-awareness is also being in touch with feelings, not letting feelings become engulfing, and having strategies to cope with moods. In her book *Molecules of Emotion*, Candace B. Pert (1998) suggests, "Feeling low and sluggish? Take a walk. Feeling anxious and jittery? Run!" (p. 293). We all need to find ways to change and manage our moods once we recognize what they are.

Managing Emotions

Managing emotions is an outcome of recognizing and labeling feelings. It is the ability to calm and soothe during anxious moments or to manage and deal with anger. Using "teachable moments" (when an inappropriate emotional response has been given), teachers can help students learn problem-solving skills to generate appropriate alternatives to the feelings. Conflict resolution is easier if students have a repertoire of strategies for dealing with conflict when it erupts.

Self-Motivation

Self-motivation consists of competencies such as persistence, setting one's own goals, and delaying gratification. Many students give up very easily when difficulties occur. Students need to feel hopeful even in the face of setback. The state of "flow" is an integral component of this domain. If students and teachers can create that state of high challenge and low threat, more learning can take place.

Empathy

Empathy is being able to feel for another. Teachers can ask students to "stand in the other person's shoes." These people may be classmates in a situation that calls for empathy. They may be characters in fiction or history with whom students can empathize to understand their emotions. This allows the students to feel how the character or individual might have felt. Understanding another's point of view or perspective is often a standard targeted in many districts. Feeling for others builds tolerance and understanding.

Social Skills

Social skills are the competencies that one uses to "read" other people and manage emotional interactions. People with high levels of social competencies have the ability to handle relationships well and are able to adapt to a variety of social situations. They are said to have "social polish." Teachers modeling these competencies and labeling them when seen in the classroom show the value of emotional intelligence in personal interactions.

The Emotional Intelligence Chart (see Figure 4) defines the five domains of emotional intelligence. It also gives suggestions for fostering each intelligence and some strategies for classroom applications.

Figure 4. Emotional Intelligence Chart

Intelligence	To Foster	Strategies for Application
Self-awareness: One's ability to sense and name a feeling when it happens	Help students discuss their feelings in different situations.	Reflection Logs and journals
Managing emotions: Recognizing and labeling feelings and responding appropriately	Use "teachable moments" to help students learn to manage emotions.	Deep breathing Counting to 10 Taking time out Physical movement
Self-motivation: Competencies such as persistence, goal setting, and delaying gratification	Help students find a niche. Help them to persist in difficult or challenging situations.	Goal setting Persistence strategies Problem solving
Empathy: Ability to feel for another person	Encourage students to "stand in another's shoes." Think about another person's pain.	Modeling empathy Discussing empathic responses to persons studied
Social skills: Competencies that one uses to "read" and manage emotional interactions	Teach social skills explicitly. Have students practice social skills while doing group tasks.	Modeling social skills Using explicit language to describe behaviors, so students can practice the skills

CLASSROOM CLIMATE

Learning Atmosphere

In a differentiated classroom, all students feel safe and secure enough to take risks and express their understanding or lack of understanding. Many times, the students considered academically gifted feel that they are expected to know all the information. Often these learners pretend to have all the answers in response to the expectations of others. This can cause stress and interfere with learning. A disappointed look or comment can keep the gifted student from expressing a lack of understanding. This student, as well as others, should feel secure in the classroom even when he or she doesn't have all the answers.

The learner who is considered to be at risk or low achieving often lives up to the expectations of the label. Giving a student a look of surprise when he "gets it" shows that he is not expected to get it! Often this puts a cap on potential. Students live up to our expectations.

In a differentiated classroom, the emphasis is on knowledge base and experience rather than IQ and ability. Each student is respected. Learners know that learning is a process and everyone learns differently. Learning includes weeding out what students know with an effective pre-assessment and determining what students need next. This policy establishes a different mind-set of being able to admit mistakes, accept lack of under-standing, and celebrate successes and growth in an individual's knowledge base. Each moment of successful improvement makes a positive change for a lifetime.

Physical and Emotional Atmosphere

The climate is influenced by the physical attributes of the classroom. Things such as appropriate lighting, cleanliness, orderliness, and displays of students' work contribute to a positive atmosphere. Plentiful and appropriate resources are necessary to facilitate student success. There could be computers and materials that allow for hands-on manipulation. There should be opportunities for social interaction and intellectual growth.

Enriched environments are created not only by materials but also by the complexity and variety of tasks and challenges and feedback (Caine & Caine, 1997; Jensen, 1998b). Engaging materials and activities help to develop *dendritic growth,* the neural connections that are facilitated by experiences and stimulation (Diamond & Hopson, 1998; Green, Greenough, & Schlumpf, 1983; Healy, 1992). As Dr. Arnold B. Scheibel, professor of neurology at UCLA, suggests,

> On the basis of what we know and have seen from animal experiments, it seems a likely inference that the same phenomenon in rats, mice, cats, and monkeys holds for humans, as well: Increase the level of environmental stimulation and challenge, and you will increase the branching of the dendrites and the thickness of the human cortex. (as cited in Diamond & Hopson, 1998, p. 35)

This growth is stimulated by a variety of complex and intriguing activities, as previously noted by Renate Caine (as cited in Healy, 1992): "If we encourage children to make choices from a selected variety of available challenges, both environmental and intellectual, we are no doubt following the wisest course" (p. 72).

Use of Music

Another component for enhancing classroom climate may be the inclusion of music. Researchers at Strathclyde University have discovered that brainpower soars when students listen to stimulating pop tunes, and they advise that playing the latest hits in classrooms may actually increase student achievement.

This study by Dr. Brian Boyd and Katrina Bowes (*The Brain in the News,* Dana Press, 2001) researched the effects of music after learning about studies in Russia that discovered that medical patients who listened to music recovered faster. In contrast to the belief that only classical music calms the learner, they found that modern music with the same tempo as classical (60 beats per minute) has the same effect and makes the mind more receptive to learning. This music can actually help the brain retain information.

Many teachers who have tried using pop music report higher levels of concentration by their students. Pop music triggers the autonomic nervous system, and we respond by feeling good and tapping our feet to the music. The pupils of the eyes dilate, and endorphin levels and energy rise. Teachers often say that students will learn more in a class if they are enjoying the experience, and music can set the stage for learning. Students will link a known routine with a piece of music and thus be ready for what is to follow. The music can be playful, for example, playing Marvin Gaye's "I Heard It Through the Grapevine" while students are estimating the number of raisins in a small, lunch-size box. Or the music can appeal to the emotions and create a mood, as happens when listening to "When Johnny Comes Marching Home Again" at the beginning of a discussion of World War I or "War," by Bruce Springsteen, in relation to the study of the Vietnam War.

Music energizes people and masks "dead air" when there is a "dip" in the energy level of students. Mozart's music or Baroque music can soothe and calm as well (Campbell, 1998).

Laughter and Celebrating Learning

Laughter is another tool to use in classrooms. It punctuates learning by releasing neuro-chemical transmitters called *endorphins,* and it is said to be the shortest distance between two people. Laughter even helps the immune system to increase the number of type T leukocytes (T cells) in the blood. T cells combat damage and infection, and some researchers have even dubbed them "happiness cells" (Cardoso, 2000). It makes sense to include humor and laughter and to celebrate learning in the classroom. Teachers can encourage students to applaud one another and cheer for each other's successes. Using energizing cheers (Burke, 1993; DePorter et al., 1998), students give rounds of applause, high fives, and other cheers that students can often create for themselves. These cheers also include actions to supplement the aural responses. Kinesthetic actions help energize students by sending more oxygen and glucose to the brain and often result in fun and laughter to raise endorphins.

Celebrating learning is important for students of all ages. A simple way to celebrate any classroom success is to lead an energizing cheer. When an individual or small group has a "lightbulb moment" or presents what has been learned, give a cheer. Besides the emotional boost, these cheers provide a physical boost to the brain. The physical actions send oxygen and glucose to the brain when arms are raised over the head and the body moves.

The following are some examples of cheers that energize and celebrate. Add your own physical movements to punctuate the cheer:

- Yes!
- Triple Yes!!!
- Oh, Yes!
- Ketchup Clap
- Fish Clap
- Table Rap Clap
- Happy Clam Clap
- Wah Hoo
- Awesome
- WOW
- Microwave
- Standing Oh!
- You Did It
- High Five
- Excellent Guitar
- Round of Applause
- You are great and getting greater!

Although each learner in the classroom is very different, everyone needs to feel safe and comfortable. In classrooms, climate and atmosphere play an important part in the learning process. Anything teachers can do to create a risk-free supportive environment where students can feel safe and where they can thrive needs to be considered and implemented in classrooms. Building a community of learners who care for and support one another is essential in a differentiated classroom. Students who know and respect each other are more tolerant of differences and more comfortable when tasks are different. Even though "one size doesn't fit all," learners require all these conditions to succeed.

1. How would you describe your classroom climate?

2. How do you encourage team building throughout the year?

3. What do you do to create an atmosphere where students can take intellectual risks in your classroom?

4. How do you create intellectual safety and prohibit ridicule, put-downs, and other negative responses in your classroom?

5. How much wait time do you allow for thinking and answering questions?

6. What steps will you take to create an inclusive atmosphere where students feel safe and included?

7. How is "relaxed alertness" created?

8. How can you create "flow"?

KNOWING THE LEARNER 3

WE LOOK IN CLASSROOMS AT SCHOOLS AND OBSERVE THE variety of students in all different shapes and sizes. They all look different, and they are. As with clothing, their sizes vary, and each wearer has individual preferences for style, color, and occasion.

Could we buy clothing for children we didn't know? We would need to find out about them as individuals, ask about their likes and dislikes, preferences for color and style, and of course their sizes. We would never consider buying just anything and hope that it would fit and appeal to the recipient. So in classrooms, we need to know the learners so that we can make sure the curriculum fits.

Many teachers have spent summers writing and designing curricula that focus on standards and are intended to engage learners. But when they met the students in the classroom, the program didn't fit their needs or appeal to them (or, it might be said, "They sent the wrong students"). It is important to look at the reality in our classrooms, recognizing that each learner is unique and that what would engage or intrigue one learner wouldn't have the slightest chance of capturing the attention of another student. Part of the reason for this situation is that students have "designer brains," as noted cognitive researcher Robert Sylwester (1995) points out. That is to say, their brains differ as much as their fingerprints and faces do. Over the years, a variety of experts have shared with educators the notion of student learning styles and the fact that we all learn in different ways, process information differently, and have distinct preferences about where, when, and how we learn.

LEARNING STYLES

How do students access, process, and express information? By viewing different theories on learning styles, personality types, and multiple intelligences, educators can learn about the individual ways in which they and their students learn and solve problems. As more information about each student's learning styles, modalities, multiple intelligences, and thinking styles is gathered, it allows teachers to use the knowledge of student strengths as an entry point for instruction and to capture attention.

It is also important for students to increase their knowledge of themselves and for teachers to help students develop metacognitive skills for self-assessment and learning for life. Knowing how one learns is necessary information if one is to learn throughout life. Research on instructional strategies at the Maryland State Department of Education indicates that "teachers who help students develop and internalize metacognitive strategies through direct instruction, modeling, and practice promote learning because the effective use of such strategies is one of the primary differences between more and less able learners" (McTighe, 1990).

One learning-styles model, developed by Rita Dunn and Ken Dunn (1987), classifies learning styles as *auditory, visual, tactile,* and *kinesthetic:*

- **Auditory Learners.** Auditory learners absorb spoken and heard material easily and like to be involved in aural questioning rather than reading materials. They prefer listening to lectures, stories, and songs, and they enjoy variation, such as voice inflection and intonational pitch. They like to discuss and use opportunities to talk about their learning with other students.

- **Visual Learners.** Visual learners learn best from information that they see or read. They like illustrations, pictures, and diagrams. Graphic organizers are useful tools for them to construct meaning visually. Color has an impact on their learning.

- **Tactile Learners.** Tactile learners learn best from handling materials, writing, drawing, and being involved with concrete experiences.

- **Kinesthetic Learners.** Kinesthetic learners learn best by doing and moving, by becoming physically involved in learning activities that are meaningful and relevant in their lives.

- **Tactile/Kinesthetic Learners.** Tactile/kinesthetic learners want to be physically involved in the learning process. They enjoy role-playing and simulations and like the freedom and opportunity to move about the classroom.

So What Should We Do About That?

It is important for teachers to be aware of the different modalities and provide adequate activities that tap into each of them during the school day.

The more teachers can involve all modalities and learning styles, the more chances they have of engaging learners in using their whole brains. Rather than trying to categorize students, it would be preferable to provide a wide range of learning activities that consider and honor each style (see Figure 5).

Examine Lesson Plans for Multiple Ways of Processing Information

Is there opportunity for auditory learners listening, speaking, and discussing?

Is the room equipped with audio headsets to provide individual time to allow students access to audiotapes, CDs, and DVDs?

Do visual learners get information from reading, observing, and viewing?

Is the room visually appealing, with charts, diagrams, pictures, and student representation for the visual learners?

Do tactile learners get a chance to examine, manipulate, and handle materials and models?

Is there ample opportunity for kinesthetic learners to move about as they need or choose to?

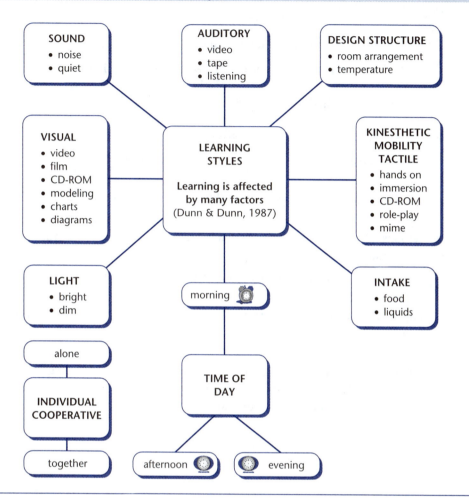

Figure 5. Learning Styles: Learning Is Affected by Such Factors as Time of Day and Environment

Do you build in role-playing and simulations that deepen understanding and satisfy the tactile-kinesthetic learners?

Variety in the classroom satisfies more learners and engages more areas of the brain, thus causing greater learning and retention.

It has been said that we learn:

10% of what we read

20% of what we hear

30% of what we see

50% of what we see and hear

70% of what is discussed with others

80% of what we experience personally, and

95% of what we teach to someone else (Ekwall & Shanker, 1988)

Teachers also need to consider other factors that affect learning styles:

- **Noise level:** Do students prefer noise or quiet?
- **Design structure:** What is the preferred room arrangement? Is the room too hot or cold?
- **Motivation and persistence:** Are they able to engage for long or short periods of time?
- **Responsibility:** Are they fairly independent and self-directed, or do they need a lot of guidance?
- **Structure:** Do they prefer to have more flexibility, or do they need detailed structure?
- **Individual/Peer:** Do they like to work with others, or do they prefer to learn alone?

Teachers also can use a learning inventory (see Figure 6) to get more data about learners and their needs. Just the knowledge that there are preferences should influence teachers' plans for presenting a variety of material and designing practice in the classroom with options and choices.

Figure 6.   How Do You Like to Learn?

1. Do you like music on while you study, or do you prefer a quiet place?
    Quiet   Music

2. Where would you prefer to work on an assignment?
    Classroom   Desk (home)
    On the floor   At a table
    On a computer

3. If you are not able to complete something, is it because
    You forgot?   You are bored?
    You got distracted?   You need help?

4. Where do you like to sit in class?
    Near the door   Front
    By the wall   Near a window
    Back

5. How do you like to work?
    _____ by yourself
    _____ with a partner
    _____ in a small group

6. Are you more alert in the afternoon? In the evening? In the morning?

7. What classes do you enjoy most and why?
    _____
    _____
    _____

8. Describe how you study. Where? When? How?
    _____
    _____
    _____

9. If you have an assignment due in 2 weeks, how do you plan to complete it?
    _____
    _____
    _____

10. If something is new for you, do you
    Like to have it explained?   Like to read about it?
    Like to watch a video/demonstration?   Like to just try it?

THINKING STYLES

Anthony Gregorc (1982), at the University of Connecticut, has developed a theory of thinking styles based on two variables: the way we view the world (whether we see the world in an abstract or concrete way) and the way we order the world (in a sequential or random order). Using these variables, Gregorc combines them to create four styles of thinking:

- **Concrete Random Thinkers.** These thinkers, who enjoy experimentation, are also known as *divergent thinkers*. They are eager to take intuitive leaps in order to create. They have a need to find alternate ways of doing things. Thus in the classroom, these types of thinkers need to be allowed to have opportunities to make choices about their learning and about how they demonstrate understandings. These learners enjoy creating new models and practical things that result from their new learning and concept development.

- **Concrete Sequential Thinkers.** These thinkers are based in the physical world identified through their senses. They are detail oriented, notice details, and recall them with ease. They require structure, frameworks, timelines, and organization to their learning. They like lecture and teacher-directed activities.

- **Abstract Sequential Thinkers.** These thinkers delight in the world of theory and abstract thought. Their thinking processes are rational, logical, and intellectual. They are happiest when involved with their own work and investigation. These learners need to have the time to examine fully the new ideas, concepts, and theories with which they have been presented. They like to support the new information by investigating and analyzing so that the learning makes sense and has real meaning for them.

- **Abstract Random Thinkers.** These thinkers organize information through sharing and discussing. They live in a world of feelings and emotion and learn best when they can personalize information. These learners like to discuss and interact with others as they learn. Cooperative group learning, centers or stations, and partner work facilitate their understanding.

Dr. Robert Sternberg, in his book *Successful Intelligence* (1996), suggests that intelligent people who will be successful in life are able to take information or knowledge and use it in practical, analytical, and creative ways. Learners with different styles bring their natural abilities to be practical, analytical, and creative to the group. Thus it is valuable to have a variety of learners' strengths working together. Different ways of thinking are not a detriment to group interaction, but rather a gift when different perspectives are represented and shared.

David Kolb (1984) also developed a learning-style profile based on experiential learning, which includes the following four groups:

- **Accommodators.** These students like to try out new things and "shake up" their own and others' "boxes." They like to be creative; they are flexible risk takers; and they want to do things "their way."

- **Convergers.** Convergers value and want to know only what is useful and relevant to the immediate situation or question. They are good at pulling out and organizing essential information. They like clear goals and specific timelines.

- **Assimilators.** These learners want to investigate, read, research, and learn as much as possible about a topic. They have the patience and tenacity to delve deeply into information, and they enjoy abstract content. They believe that they learn from past experiences and from experts.

- **Divergers.** These students value positive, caring environments where their surroundings are comfortable. They like to learn from others through conversation and dialogue. They want to explore and seek alternatives, and they are altruistic in their pursuit of learning.

Bernice McCarthy's 4MAT model (McCarthy, 1990; McCarthy & McCarthy, 2006) identifies four learning styles and the type of teaching strategies best suited to each of them: (1) the imaginative learner, (2) the analytical learner, (3) the commonsense learner, and (4) the dynamic learner. Learners are capable of working in all four areas some of the time, but most of us tend to favor one style over all others. The trick for teachers is to provide experiences in the four areas to accommodate all learners and to increase their range of learning styles. It can be useful to view the model as a circle divided into four quadrants that can be used to guide lesson planning and teaching (see Figure 7).

Figure 7. Learners Tend to Favor One Particular Learning Style But Are Capable of Working in All Four Areas, as Suggested by Bernice McCarthy's 4MAT Model (McCarthy 1990; McCarthy & McCarthy, 2006)

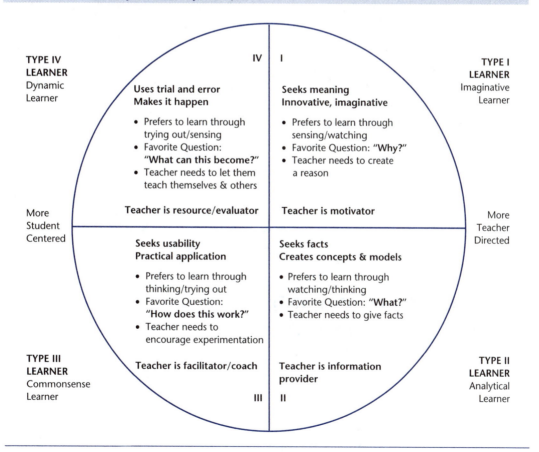

- **Type 1: The Imaginative Learner (Experiencing).** This type of learner seeks meaning. Type 1 learners are innovative and imaginative, preferring to learn through feeling and reflecting. Their teachers need to create a reason and provide a rationale for the learning that connects to their own lives and has relevance. Positive relationships and nurturing teachers are important aspects that need to be present in classrooms.

- **Type 2: The Analytical Learner (Conceptualizing).** This type of learner seeks facts. Type 2 learners prefer to learn by watching and thinking. They create concepts and models. They appreciate information and teacher lectures.

- **Type 3: The Commonsense Learner (Applying).** This type of learner seeks usability and practical application and prefers to learn through thinking and trying out. Experimentation and problem solving are processes that intrigue this learner.

- **Type 4: The Dynamic Learner (Creating).** These learners seek to learn through trial and error and prefer to learn by trying out and sensing. They want to teach themselves and others and to use the teacher as a resource. They are risk takers and prefer self-discovery, disliking rigid routines and methodical tasks.

Silver, Strong, and Perini (2000) outline a model of four learning styles derived from the theories of Carl Jung and Isabel Briggs Myers:

- **Self-Expressive Learners.** These learners prefer opportunities for original, flexible, and elaborative thinking. They appreciate teachers who give them choices and facilitate their learning. They are innovative, creative learners.

- **Mastery Learners.** These learners prefer opportunities to observe, describe, memorize, and practice new learning to reach mastery. They appreciate teachers who present information and arrange for practice. They enjoy developing mastery of basic skills.

- **Understanding Learners.** These learners prefer opportunities to summarize, classify, compare, contrast, and look for cause and effect. They appreciate teachers who provide information and then probe for explanations and reasons behind the facts. They think logically and analytically, seeking evidence to support their learning.

- **Interpersonal Learners.** These learners prefer opportunities to socialize, describe feelings, empathize, and provide support and approval. They appreciate teachers who relate the content to them personally so that they can recognize relevance and add meaning to their work.

USING LEARNING AND THINKING STYLES IN THE CLASSROOM

The connections and similarities between and among these various learning styles can be compared using a matrix (see Figure 8). Vertically, each column outlines a different research interpretation. Horizontally, each row shows how the different perspectives align with each other.

Harvey Silver and colleagues often use metaphorical thinking in their workshops. The analogous use of four items with which most people are familiar (a beach ball, clipboard, microscope, and puppy) can help learners understand the attributes of each style

Figure 8.	A Matrix of Learning Styles Illustrates Their Connections and Similarities			
	Gregorc	**Kolb**	**Silver/Strong/ Hanson**	**4MAT/ McCarthy**
Beach Ball	**Concrete Random** Divergent Experiential Inventive	**Accommodator** Likes to try new ideas. Values creativity, flexibility, and risk takers.	**Self-Expressive** Feelings to construct new ideas. Produces original and unique materials.	**Type 4 Dynamic** Create and act. Usefulness and application of learning.
Clipboard	**Concrete Sequential** Task oriented Efficient Detailed	**Converger** Values what is useful and relevant, immediacy, and organizing essential information.	**Mastery** Absorbs information concretely, and processes step by step.	**Type 3 Commonsense** Think and do. Active, practical. Make things work.
Microscope	**Abstract Sequential** Intellectual Analytical Theoretical	**Assimilator** Avid readers who seek to learn. Patience for research. Values concepts.	**Understanding** Prefers to explore ideas and use reason and logic based on evidence.	**Type 2 Analytical** Reflect and think. Observers who appreciate lecture methods.
Puppy	**Abstract Random** Imaginative Emotional Holistic	**Diverger** Values positive, caring environments that are attractive, comfortable, and people oriented.	**Interpersonal** Appreciates concrete ideas and social interaction to process and use knowledge.	**Type 1 Imaginative** Feel and reflect. Create and reflect on an experience.

and to remember that style by recalling those attributes that relate to the familiar items. Making students aware of these styles, perhaps by asking them about the attributes of beach balls, clipboards, microscopes, and puppies, and having them brainstorm those characteristics will help students understand the differences between styles in the classroom.

After the brainstorming, students can link the profiles to what would be important to provide for these types of learners in the classroom in order for them to be successful in school. For example, beach balls would want to keep moving, be creative, and be free to go where they wish. Therefore if they were in a classroom at school, they would like choice and options in their learning and to have the opportunity to be creative and move freely, using centers and so forth. Students can rank these four items or symbols from 1 to 4, depending on their understanding of themselves. Teachers can point out that we all have some characteristics of each type but that students' top two choices show the way they would prefer to learn and the types of activities that would be most comfortable for them.

Teachers may want to take time to examine what each of the four symbols could appreciate in the classroom. One group of teachers generated the following list, containing things that they thought the four types would value in the classroom:

Beach Ball

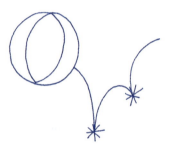

- Variety of resources
- Adaptive environment
- Various manipulatives
- Choice of activities
- Spontaneity
- Extensions to activities
- Personal freedom

Clipboard

- Organization
- Structure
- Visual directions
- Clear closure
- Sequential learning
- Clear procedures
- Consistent routines
- Clear expectations

Microscope

- Investigative learning
- Critical thinking
- Verifying information
- Analyzing concepts
- Deep exploration
- Discussions

- Focus on details
- Ownership

Puppy

- Comfortable environment
- Encouraging atmosphere
- Supportive grouping
- Safe climate
- Respectful colleagues
- Empathic listeners
- Sensitive peers

It is not as important which style delineator a teacher uses as it is that the teacher recognize the fact that different students have different preferences. The teacher must design the learning so that the diverse populations in the classroom all have their needs satisfied at some point.

MULTIPLE INTELLIGENCES

Howard Gardner's (1983) theory of multiple intelligences provides us with another frame through which we can observe students and understand how they learn and process information:

> It is of the utmost importance that we recognize and nurture all of the varied human intelligences, and all of the combinations of intelligences. We are all so different largely because we all have different combinations of intelligences. If we recognize this, I think we will have at least a better chance of dealing appropriately with the many problems that we face in the world. (Gardner, 1983)

Gardner offers us eight ways of being smart:

1. Verbal/Linguistic: reading, writing, speaking, and listening

2. Logical/Mathematical: working with numbers and abstract patterns

3. Visual/Spatial: working with graphic images, mind mapping, graphic organizers, visualizing, drawing, and exploring the world of color and art

4. Musical/Rhythmic: using rhythm, melody, patterned sound, song, rap, dance

5. Bodily/Kinesthetic: processing information through touch, movement, dramatics, manipulatives, and using a variety of fine and gross motor skills in everyday life

6. Interpersonal: sharing, cooperating, interviewing, relating, and brainstorming with others

7. Intrapersonal: working alone, self-paced instruction, individualized projects, and metacognitive thinking

8. Naturalist: spending time outdoors, sorting, classifying, and noticing patterns in the world

Finding Gold

One teacher shared with us that she felt she was constantly observing her students trying to identify their strengths in multiple intelligences. She likened it to "mining for gold." Teachers in classrooms have been not only recognizing the various intelligences that students possess but also consciously providing learning experiences that include more than the most frequently used verbal and logical intelligences. They consider the notion that when we want to "catch fish," we bait the hook with what the fish like, not what the fisherman likes. So in classrooms, teachers should use a variety of teaching and learning strategies as "bait" that will appeal to the learners, not just to the teacher.

"Kidwatching"

Getting to know students is one way of gathering data to build learning profiles for each student. Teachers and students need to know their strengths to enhance self-confidence as well as areas that need improvement, so goal setting and metacognition can be implemented. Teachers and students may use checklists and questionnaires (see Figures 9 through 14) to gain insight into students' preferred areas of multiple intelligences.

How Are You Intelligent?

"How Are You Intelligent?" (see Figure 9) is a checklist that students and teachers may use to increase personal awareness and understanding of areas of strength, which will increase self-awareness and confidence, and to identify areas that they may need to target for growth. Students may check off the items that are most like themselves and then transfer that information to a bar graph, filling in one cube in each row for each item checked in each intelligence category. The bar graph can then be cut to create each student's "Unique Individual Profile" (see Figure 10), which may be used to compare and contrast their profiles with other students with whom they may be working (Fogarty & Stoehr, 1995). This helps students recognize that together they have at least three or four areas of strength and therefore more tools for creativity and problem solving. This activity reinforces the notion that our diversity is our strength. As students learn through experience and reflection on those experiences, their profiles will be forever changing (see also Chapman, 1993).

Student Observations

Observing students as they work and interact helps us to know them better. Some classroom teachers set up areas where students choose games or activities for leisure time at noon hour or recess. The types of games they choose gives teachers information about their preferences. For example, some students choose games or activities that involve words and letters, others problems and logic, others creative options, and still others social interaction. Teachers often use clipboards and self-sticking notes to capture observations about students that can be transferred into student profiles (see Figure 11) whenever possible.

Figure 9. How Are You Intelligent?	
VERBAL/LINGUISTIC INTELLIGENCE • I like to tell jokes, tell stories or tales. • Books are important to me. • I like to read. • I often listen to radio, TV, tapes, or CDs. • I write easily and enjoy it. • I quote things I've read. • I like crosswords and word games.	**INTRAPERSONAL INTELLIGENCE** • I know about my feelings, strengths, and weaknesses. • I like to learn more about myself. • I enjoy hobbies by myself. • I enjoy being alone sometimes. • I have confidence in myself. • I like to work alone. • I think about things and plan what to do next.
LOGICAL/MATHEMATICAL INTELLIGENCE • I solve math problems easily. • I enjoy math and using computers. • I like strategy games. • I wonder how things work. • I like using logic to solve problems. • I reason things out. • I like to use data in my work to measure, calculate, and analyze.	**VISUAL/SPATIAL INTELLIGENCE** • I shut my eyes and see clear pictures. • I think in pictures. • I like color and interesting designs. • I can find my way around unfamiliar areas. • I draw and doodle. • I like books with pictures, maps, and charts. • I like videos, movies, and photographs.
INTERPERSONAL INTELLIGENCE • People ask me for advice. • I prefer team sports. • I have many close friends. • I like working in groups. • I'm comfortable in a crowd. • I have empathy for others. • I can figure out what people are feeling.	**BODILY/KINESTHETIC INTELLIGENCE** • I get uncomfortable when I sit too long. • I like to touch or be touched when talking. • I use my hand when speaking. • I like working with my hands on crafts/hobbies. • I touch things to learn more about them. • I think of myself as well coordinated. • I learn by doing rather than watching.
MUSICAL/RHYTHMIC INTELLIGENCE • I like to listen to musical selections. • I am sensitive to music and sounds. • I can remember tunes. • I listen to music when studying. • I enjoy singing. • I keep time to music. • I have a good sense of rhythm.	**NATURALIST** • I enjoy spending time in nature. • I like to classify things into categories. • I can hear animal and bird sounds clearly. • I see details when I look at plants, flowers, and trees. • I am happiest outdoors. • I like tending to plants and animals. • I know the names of trees, plants, birds, and animals.

Figure 10.	What Is Your Unique Multiple Intelligences Profile?							
Word Smart								
Math Smart								
People Smart								
Music Smart								
Self Smart								
Picture Smart								
Body Smart								
Nature Smart								

SOURCE: Adapted with permission from *Integrating Curricula With Multiple Intelligences: Teams, Themes, and Threads*, by Robin Fogarty and Judy Stoehr. © 1995 Corwin Press. www.corwinpress.com.

Figure 11. Teachers Can Capture Observations Over Time About Students'
Multiple Intelligences and Transfer Them to Student Profiles

Student Profile

Observing over time . . .	Name:
Verbal/Linguistic	Intrapersonal
Logical/Mathematical	Visual/Spatial
Interpersonal	Bodily/Kinesthetic
Musical/Rhythmic	Naturalist

Logs and Journals

Teachers gain valuable information in logs and journals in which students reflect on their learning and their enjoyment or preference of one learning activity over another. Having students use exit passes as they leave the class can give the teacher immediate feedback on specific topics. Just asking students what they enjoyed, or learned best from, or didn't appreciate gives information that can be valuable in future planning. Teachers can also check for clarification and understanding of material that was examined in class that day by asking what was clear, what was unclear, or what questions still need clarification. Figure 12 offers a self-reflection tool that students can use in journals as a whole or as individual items over several days.

In early elementary classrooms, students can use symbols or a "Yes—Maybe—No" checklist (see Figure 13) instead of words to indicate their preferences. The teacher may pose questions like those listed on the bottom half of the checklist, and after thinking about each question, the students can draw a face on the appropriate line that shows how they feel about the activity.

As teachers become more aware of students' unique learning styles and intelligences, they become more able to design learning experiences that appeal to their students' different needs and interests. Because teachers are also unique individuals who tend to have styles of teaching that fit their personal profiles, it is often a stretch to include instructional and assessment tools and strategies that are not in their personal comfort zones.

Teachers need to build repertoires that will engage more learners and honor the diversity in each classroom. The multiple intelligences offer many options for including all eight, where appropriate, in lessons (see Figure 14). When teachers use a variety of multiple intelligences processes, they offer diverse learners more opportunities to learn and to show what they know in many ways. Refer to the palette of suggestions to guide lesson planning (see Figure 15).

Teachers continually gather data and observe students as the students become more familiar with their unique ways of learning. Teachers then can consciously include a variety of learning and assessment experiences that would appeal and engage a greater number of students. Students will then feel challenged in areas they feel confident pursuing. We realize that with individual learning styles and multiple intelligences profiles, one size of learning could not possibly fit everyone in the classroom. Knowing the learners and consciously and strategically planning to address their styles, intelligences, and learning preferences will increase the chances of engaging them and offering a variety of ways to learn.

Figure 12. Eight Intelligences: Self-Reflection Tool
Used by Students Individually or With Peers

Complete this page and compare your answers with your partner.

If I could do anything I like, I'd . . . .

Usually, when I have free time I . . . .

My hobbies are . . . .

At school I like to . . . .

The type of things that we do in class I really like are . . . .

I am uncomfortable when people ask me to . . . .

Do you like to work alone or with a group? Why?

Figure 13.   Yes—Maybe—No Line

1.

2.

3.

4.

5.

6.

7.

8.

9.

10.

Ask students about a variety of activities that they might have the opportunity to do.

How do you feel about . . .

1. Drawing and artwork?

2. Musical activities?

3. Working with others?

4. Working alone?

5. Using numbers?

6. Writing? Talking?

7. Dancing, sports, moving while learning?

8. Solving problems?

9. Reading?

10. Thinking about things?

11. Working with technology?

12. Being a leader?

Figure 14.   Focusing on Multiple Intelligences in the Classroom

Definitions	Cultivation of Intelligence	Applications in Classroom
Verbal/Linguistic Uses language to read, write, and speak to communicate	• Play word games for vocabulary • Practice explaining ideas • Tell jokes and riddles • Play trivia games • Make up limericks	Write Report Explain Describe and discuss Interview Label Give and follow directions
Musical/Rhythmic Communicates in rhyme and rhythm	• Interview people about their favorite music • Make up a song about your favorite things • Play "name that tune" • Create a class song • Share poems that are special to you	Chant Sing Raps and songs Beat a rhythm Poetry Limericks
Logical/ Mathematical Uses logic and reason to solve problem	• Introduce graphic organizers to students and let them reflect on their use • Offer logic problems or situations and have students share problem-solving strategies	Advance organizers Graphic organizers Puzzles Debates Critical thinking Graphs and charts Data and statistics
Visual/Spatial Ability to visualize in the mind's eye	• Offer students opportunities to close their eyes and visualize: scenes, processes, and events • Allow and encourage students to add drawings and representations in their work or demonstrate understanding	Draw Create Visualize Paint Imagine Models Describe in detail
Bodily/Kinesthetic Ability to learn and express oneself through the whole body	• Let students role-play processes and events • Create a dance or mime to illustrate new learning • Create gestures or actions that demonstrate new learning	Perform Create Construct Develop Manipulate Dance or mime
Naturalist Ability to recognize and classify	• Provide students with opportunities to classify and examine learning for similar or different attributes • Allow students time for examination and a closer look	Classify, sort Organize using criteria Investigate Analysis Identify, categorize
Intrapersonal Ability to be self-reflective	• Ask students to think about a plan for their assignment or to reflect on the process and set goals for improvement • Introduce journals or reflection time so students reflect on their work and their thinking	Metacognition Logs and journals Independent study Goal setting Positive affirmations Autobiography Personal questions
Interpersonal Ability to work with others	• Practice positive skills of active listening, encouragement • Show appreciation for the "smarts" of others	Group work Partner activities Reciprocal teaching Peer reading, editing, counseling Role-playing Class meetings Conferencing and sharing

Figure 15.   Suggestions for Using the Eight Multiple Intelligences

Verbal/Linguistic

Brainstorming.
Organizing thoughts.
Summarize.
Change the beginning or the end.
Describe it.
Write an advertisement.
Write an editorial.
Write a news flash.
Prepare a speech.
Develop a campaign platform.
Develop a challenging question.
Find evidence to support a claim or belief.
This is like _____ because _____.
Research the inventor or an author.
Write a conclusion, summary.
Write main idea and supporting details.
Develop a book.
Record reading or writing.
Skim and scan.
Write the attributes.
Write adjectives or
    phrases to describe.

Musical/Rhythmic

Create a song.
Think of a theme song and say why.
Write a poem.
Create a jingle or slogan.
Select sounds to fit.
Recognize pitch, tone, timbre.
Use background music.
Create a beat.
Make rhythmic movements.
Identify sounds.
Identify musical pieces.
Interpret a song.
Record music.
Develop an instrument.
Find the background music.

Logical/Mathematical

Sequence it.
Design a game.
Develop a TV show.
Create a timeline.
Tell your process.
Categorize.
Find the missing piece or link.
Classify.
Rank ideas.
Use a matrix.
Design a graph.
Try a new idea against a model.
Survey.
Conduct an inventory.
Research and gather data.
Interpret data.
Technology world.
Gadget use.
Compute or calculate.
Use deductive thinking.
Use numbers.

Visual/Spatial

Draw a picture or graphic.
Make a flip book.
Create a photo essay.
Design a poster.
Design a puppet.
Depict the setting.
Make a collage.
Illustrate it.
Plot on a graphic organizer.
Design or create.
Associations, recognitions, and use of color.
Use different art media.
Interpreting of art.
Design a book.
Sculpt it!
Draw a map and label sites of importance.
Develop a diorama.
Design a collage.
Highlight or tabbing.
Develop a character sketch.
Develop an editorial cartoon.
Write a cartoon strip with speech bubbles.
Color code.

Figure 15.   (Continued)

Bodily/Kinesthetic

Movement.
Name its function.
Brainstorm.
Use your body to interpret meaning.
Play a game or sport.
Use manipulative.
Construct or build.
Role-play.
Perform.
Act it out.
Mime.
Puppet show.
Show how you know.
Dramatize.
Create simulations.
Interpretive dance.
Do an experiment.
Invent or discover through
    trial and error.

Interpersonal

Work with others.
Empathetic with others.
Work on a group project.
Conduct an interview.
Discuss with others.
Be involved in a conversation.
Come to a consensus.
Give or receive feedback.
Jigsaw information.
Be a team member.

Intrapersonal

Select personal choice.
Work alone.
Metacognitive thinking.
Plan a way.
Get a strategy.
Draw a conclusion of how it
    makes you feel.
Identify likes and dislikes.
Make choices.
Set goals.
Carry through a task.
How does it feel?
Identify your personal preference.
Automaticity.

Naturalist

Surviving.
Understanding nature.
Use nature to work for you.
The study of science.
Apply information to life.
Make a personal link and connection from
    your world.
Survival needs and awareness of them.
Identify scientific method and
    classifications.
Study of land, sea, and air.
Making discoveries.
Inventing.
Exploring the world.

Chapter 3Reflections

1. How do you get to know your students? What methods do you use?

2. How do you stimulate your students' strongest intelligences? How do you encourage students to cultivate their other intelligences?

3. How could you develop awareness about multiple intelligences with students and parents?

4. Use the checklist on the lesson planner to check that learning styles and multiple intelligences are varied.

JUST AS ONE SIZE OF LEARNING DOESN'T FIT ALL, ONE SIZE OF assessment doesn't suit, either. We can hold up clothing to see how it might look, but until we put it on, we don't know what changes need to be made. We may need a new size or a different style or color. So in assessing the learning, we need different approaches to check the fit and adjust the learning.

We in education tend to banter about the terms *assessment, evaluation,* and *grading* without necessarily having clearly distinctive definitions for each term. *Assessment* is often referred to as the gathering of data; *evaluation* is the judging of merits; and *grading* is assigning values to letters or numbers for reporting purposes (Rolheiser, Bower, & Stevahn, 2000).

Assessment as ongoing feedback is a necessary component of the learning process, not something that happens at the end of the learning. It has been said that feedback is often too little, too late, too vague, presented in the wrong form, and therefore lacking in impact (Jensen, 1998a, p. 54). Our challenge is to find ways to facilitate ongoing feedback for students that will increase their chances to continue to grow and improve their learning.

One of the first things that needs to be done is pre-assessment, to find out what students already know or can do.

It takes time to do quality pre-assessments, but it can be a very worthwhile process. Planning for individual needs is easier when the teacher knows what a student knows, how the student feels about the topic, and what he or she is interested in learning during the study.

PURPOSES OF PRE-ASSESSMENT

Assessing student knowledge prior to the learning experience helps the teacher find out

- What the student already knows about the unit being planned
- What standards, objectives, concepts, and skills the individual student understands
- What further instruction and opportunities for mastery are needed
- What requires reteaching or enhancement
- What areas of interests and feelings are in the different areas of the study
- How to set up flexible groups: **T (total), A (alone), P (partner), S (small) group**

When teaching with high achievement as a goal, one important aspect of assessing learners is finding out what the students already know. This knowledge is based on their prior learning and experiences. By doing a pre-assessment of knowledge, teachers can plan curriculum and design instruction to meet the needs of the total class as well as individuals. The written tests are one form of pre-assessment.

Try this handy tip! Administer the pretest 2 or 3 weeks before the information is to be taught. The test needs to vary in types of questions for an accurate assessment. That gives the teacher time to plan for the novice to the expert and those along the way. By administering the test early, the seeds of excitement have been planted about all the interesting things the students will be learning. Students need to realize that through experiences, one learns. They may be at a novice level of knowing because of lack of experience and opportunity. This is sometimes difficult for a student to admit. One must realize that the pre-assessment tools provide information for planning what the individual needs and that no one is expected to be at the expert level in everything being taught.

When learners know the information, they may be allowed to move on to another dimension of the unit of study. For those who have not had exposure to the information prior to the pre-assessment, this allows the teacher to provide an experience for them.

One way to get this point across to students is to name some sports, hobbies, or free-time favorites and find those who are experienced and those who do not know much about them. These students have other areas of interests and expertise. We are all smart, just in different ways. For instance, a star football player knows all the plays of the game and practices for hours. Some of us who attend the football games know the basic rules, and then there are others who do not know anything about the game of football. This has nothing to do with their intelligence; it has to do with their experience, their talents, their interests, and being in the right place at the right time.

Some children in first grade may be having difficulty with the concepts for adding and subtracting numbers. Yet when you get to the money unit, you find that they have been going to the store, spending money, and getting change. These children are in fact able to use the principles of adding and subtracting. Experience and survival have taught them this. Other students may not have had these same experiences.

Pretest

- Cover whole unit of group.
- Include simple-to-complex and concrete-to-abstract understandings.
- Arrange test questions in groupings that relate to the same standards so that the data, when examined, will clearly indicate knowledge or gaps in knowledge.
- Recall facts.
- Ask students to use the information to show another way, form, or situation.
- Interpret information such as charts and graphs.
- Allow drawing, interpreting, or demonstrating.
- Ask open-ended questions to elicit more information.

Informal Pre-Assessment

- Demonstrate with manipulatives, if appropriate, to show application.
- Use interest surveys.

- Use dialogue to find out what students want to learn and how they feel about the topic.
- Analyze the pretest data so you can make planning decisions.

Rank Scores

- Determine appropriate uses of flexible grouping.
- Form timelines for the unit of study or topic.
- Discover the number of students at different levels of mastery.
- The teacher is then able to identify and determine what level of mastery students have reached for the standards, concepts, and skills that will be taught:
  - Beyond expectation (understand, apply, can transfer to other situations)
  - Mastered (a basic understanding)
  - Approaching mastery
  - Introductory, novice, or beginning stage

Then a learning plan can be developed for students at each level of mastery.

There are other effective tools and strategies to use to pre-assess students' knowledge. Emotions and feelings play a large role in the way in which a student learns information. When a person has had a bad experience in the past and is learning or doing something that triggers that memory, there is a barrier formed that inhibits the new learning. When the experience is a quality one with a purpose, a positive impact, and a great experience, the learner feels open to learning more and experiencing more with the topic. These pre-assessment tools relate feelings, emotional links, and knowledge gathered from past experiences. This can have a strong impact on the present learning. The following are some examples of more informal pre-assessment tools that can be used at the beginning of lessons to open mental files and find out students' predispositions.

SAMPLES OF INFORMAL PRE-ASSESSMENTS

Squaring Off

This very successful pre-assessment tool involves the total group.

1. Place a card in each corner of the room with one of the following words or phrases, which are effective ways to group according to learner knowledge (see Figures 16 and 17):

Rarely ever	Sometimes	Often	I have it!
Dirt road	Paved road	Highway	Yellow Brick Road
I know very little	I know some	I know a lot	I know all about this!

2. Tell the students to go to the corner of the room that matches their place in the learning journey.

3. Participants go to the corner of the room that most closely matches their own learning status and discuss what they know about the topic or event and why they chose to go there.

Figure 16.   Squaring Off Sample at Sea

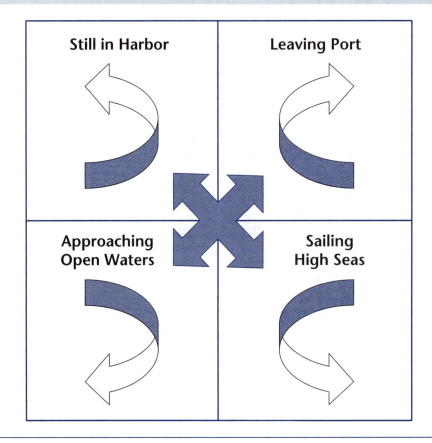

Boxing

1. Getting to the Heart of the Matter

   Draw a box in the center of a piece of paper. Draw a smaller box inside the first box.

   - Outside Box:
     What do I know about this topic?

   - Inside Box:
     What do I want to learn? or
     What is my goal?

2. Gift of Success

   - Outside Box: Write one of the following:
     What else do I know about this topic?
     How does it fit?
     What does this have to do with _____?

Figure 17.   Squaring Off Sample on Land

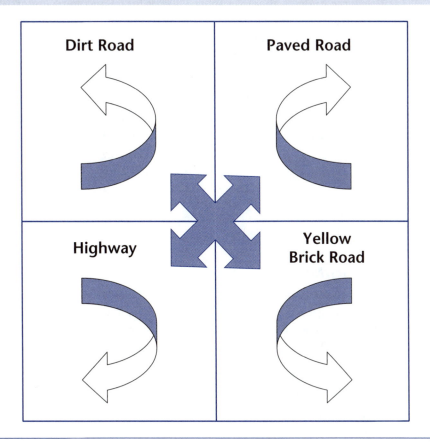

Dirt Road

Paved Road

Highway

Yellow
Brick Road

- Inside Box:
  Draw a model or picture of the topic.
  Create graphic organizer to explain the topic.
- Middle of the Box:
  Summarize: Write a sentence to explain your thinking.

Yes/No Cards

Yes/No cards may be set up as one-sided cards or two-sided cards.

Using One-Sided Yes/No Cards

- Give students two blank note cards or pieces of paper. Ask them to write YES on one and NO on the other.
- When a question is asked, the students should hold up a card—YES if they understand, NO if they do not understand.

Examples:

1. Ask the students about vocabulary words for an upcoming unit. Give the word and ask students to show the YES card if they know the word and its definition and show the NO card if they do not know the word and its definition.

2. Ask someone who is showing a YES card to define the word. This way, the students realize you will be checking their responses.

3. Use some of the most interesting information and words from the upcoming unit to build up anticipation about the topic.

4. Remind students that if they do not know these words, they will be learning more about them in the upcoming unit.

- Get creative and customize phrases for your class to write on the cards. Some alternative phrases and symbols might be: Got It! (yes) and Not a Clue (no), or plus (yes) and minus (no) signs.

Using Two-Sided Yes/No Cards

Teachers may prefer to use two-sided Yes/No cards. In this case, students or teachers can prepare the cards, writing Yes at the top of each card and No underneath it on both sides of the card. When the teacher asks the question, the student holds up the card, pinching the side of the card next to the selected answer. Advantages of two-sided cards include:

- When the student holds up the Yes/No card, everyone in the class can view the correct answer on both sides of the card.

- The student can view both Yes and No answers before responding to the teacher's question.

- The teacher can assess the student's finger movements. For example, some students will go right for the answer and pinch, while others move their fingers back and forth, deciding which one is the correct answer. This shows the teacher who is secure and knows the answer and who is still unsure.

Examples of Yes/No Cards for the Content Areas

Yes/No cards can also be customized to show subject-specific concepts in the content areas. Examples include:

Math

- add, subtract, multiply, divide
- square, circle, trapezoid, rectangle
- prime, composite

Social Studies

- Asia, Africa, North America
- plebeians, counsel, dictator
- north, south, east, west
- farm, desert, rain forest

Science

- invertebrate, vertebrate
- land, sea, air
- hypothesis, problem, conclusion
- sink, float

Language Arts

- explicit, implicit
- noun, verb, adjective
- nonfiction, fiction
- subject, predicate

Arts and Music

- classical, disco, country
- string, percussion, horn
- renaissance, baroque, modern
- watercolor, oils, chalk

All Subjects

- cause, effect
- fact, opinion
- beginning, middle, end
- understand, do not understand
- yes, no, some
- happy, so-so, sad

Graffiti Fact

Create a "Graffiti Board of Facts." Post all the things the class knows about the topic of study:

- What we knew
- What we learned
- What we want to learn next

Give students time to process and think about the answers. Encourage them to write down their answers before sharing with the group. Let students answer the questions alone at first and jot down their answers. In addition, urge students to write their own answers on the Graffiti Board of Facts to foster ownership of the answers.

SURVEYS AT WORK

Construct Quality Surveys

Teachers know the goal, the purpose, and the information that is to be learned. Survey often, because students' interests change as they grow. These tools will teach you so much about the learners in your classroom!

The surveys may help you find out about the preknowledge or experience that students have with an upcoming unit (content survey). They may help you design performance tasks related to their preferences or ratings (preference or interest surveys). They also may give you suggestions for classroom configuration and grouping (social surveys).

Sample Interest Survey Questions

	Rarely Ever	Sometimes	Most of the Time
1. I like to make up songs.	_____	_____	_____
2. I like to try things that are hard to do.	_____	_____	_____
3. Brain puzzles hold my interest.	_____	_____	_____
4. I like to take things apart and assemble them.	_____	_____	_____
5. I enjoy creating.	_____	_____	_____
6. I need manipulatives to learn.	_____	_____	_____
7. I am a follower.	_____	_____	_____
8. I am a leader.	_____	_____	_____
9. I prefer to work alone.	_____	_____	_____
10. I like to read.	_____	_____	_____
11. I prefer to work with others.	_____	_____	_____
12. I like to draw my own pictures.	_____	_____	_____
13. I can see visual images in my head.	_____	_____	_____
14. I have at least one pet.	_____	_____	_____
15. I enjoy animals.	_____	_____	_____
16. I would rather be outside than inside.	_____	_____	_____
17. I would rather be inside than outside.	_____	_____	_____
18. I like school.	_____	_____	_____
19. I do not like school.	_____	_____	_____
20. School would be better if . . .	_____	_____	_____
21. If I have free time, I prefer to	_____	_____	_____
a. _____	_____	_____	_____
b. _____	_____	_____	_____
c. _____	_____	_____	_____
22. I do not like _____ because _____.	_____	_____	_____
23. Additional Comments	_____	_____	_____
a. _____	_____	_____	_____
b. _____	_____	_____	_____

Math Interest Survey

Name: _____

Address: _____

Home Phone:_____

Date: _____

Course: _____

Please help me to get to know you better.

1. My top 2 or 3 favorite activities are _____

2. Other activities that I like to do are _____

3. My favorite subject is _____

4. In my free time, I _____

5. On TV, I like to watch _____

6. The music I listen to is _____

7. I think a teacher should _____ and _____

8. My favorite movies are _____ and _____

9. I like my family because _____

10. I dislike school because _____

11. I like school because _____

12. Friends are important because _____

13. The most interesting person whom I have met is _____ because
    _____

14. My chores at home are _____

15. My job outside of school is _____. How often? _____

16. I volunteer at _____. How often? _____

17. If I had $500, I would _____

18. I am in this math class because _____

19. I think this class will be (easy/difficult) because _____

20. I am excited about this class because _____

21. I am fearful of this class because _____

22. The things I will do in this class to be successful are _____

23. The things that may prevent me from being successful are _____

24. Something that I want you to know about me is _____

25. Any additional comments: _____

Foreign Language Interest Inventory (Getting to Know You)

Name: _____

Age: _____

Date: _____

Class: _____

Please help me to get to know you better.

1. My top 2 or 3 favorite activities are _____

2. Other activities that I like to do are _____

3. My favorite subject is _____

4. In my free time, I _____

5. On TV, I like to watch _____

6. The music I listen to is _____

7. I think a teacher should _____ and _____

8. My favorite movies are _____ and _____

9. I like my family because _____

10. I dislike school because _____

11. I like school because _____

12. Friends are important because _____

13. The most interesting person whom I have met is _____

14. My chores at home are _____

15. If I had $500, I would _____

16. I am in this Spanish class because _____

17. I think this class will be (easy/difficult) because _____

18. I am excited about this class because _____

19. I am fearful of this class because _____

20. The things I will do in this class to be successful are _____

21. The things that may prevent me from being successful are _____

22. Something that I want you to know about me is _____

23. Any additional comments: _____

Pre-Assessment of Content Survey

Directions: Write what you know about each of the topics about the country of _____. We will be studying this soon.

Focus: Study of a Country Such as Canada or Mexico

- History
- Industry
- Beliefs
- Government
- Celebrations, festivals, holidays, and rites
- Geography and location

Students may use a grid to organize their information and use pictures, symbols, and words.

History	Industry	Beliefs
Government	Celebrations	Geography

A "Four-Corner Pre-Assessment" may be used to find out or assess a student's prior knowledge. The following example is only one way to get information. You could put any questions in the grid that would give you the information you want. This may be given out as a ticket a week or two before the unit of study would commence.

Something you know about reptiles.	What are two questions about reptiles?
What would be a good project about reptiles?	With whom would you like to work?

ASSESSMENT TOOLS TO USE DURING THE LEARNING

As students are working, we need to offer opportunities for feedback from teachers, from peers, and through self-reflection. Without feedback, people cannot improve. If we wait until the end of the learning, it may be too late and incorrect information or skills may have been developed. The following strategies are engaging ways to assess student progress informally throughout the learning process.

Thumb It

Have students respond with the position of their thumbs to get an assessment of their understanding.

Where am I now in my understanding of _____?

a. Upside   b. Onside (sideways)   c. Downside

Know a lot   Know some   Know very little

Fist of Five

Have students use their hands to show their levels of understanding. Showing all five fingers indicates the highest level of understanding.

How well do I know this?

1 2 3 4 5

5. I know it so well, I could explain it to anyone.

4. I can do it alone.

3. I need some help.

2. I could use more practice.

1. I am beginning to understand.

Face the Fact

Happy   **Straight**   **Sad**

1. Have students draw a happy face, a straight face, and a sad face on individual note cards.

2. State a fact related to the topic that can be answered with an emotion.

3. Ask students to hold up the card that matches the emotion.

4. Make motions with your hands to imitate the facial emotions. Curve up for the happy face, flat for the straight face, or curve down for the sad face.

Reaching for the Top

1. Tell the students to extend one arm straight up in the air.

2. Instruct students to move the opposite hand up that arm as if it were a gauge marked with a 2–4–6–8 scale. Number 2 is at the shoulder, numbers 4 and 6 moving up the arm, and number 8 is at the fingers pointing to the ceiling. This makes learning a cheer celebration!

As the student positions his or her hand against the upraised arm, do a quick scan of the class to check for understanding.

Speedometer Reading

1. Tell students to imagine the speedometer on a car or draw one on the board. Explain that the speedometer tells how fast the car is moving. The car starts off at zero miles per hour. Its maximum speed is 100 miles per hour.

2. Have students lay one arm on top of the other with hands touching elbows.

3. Ask students to move the arm that is on top to show a "speed" between 0 and 100. Students show how well they understand or how much they know by indicating the speed on the dial. For example, the student who understands a lot will show 100 miles per hour. The student who knows a little might show 30 miles per hour. Gauge students' understanding by checking the speedometers.

REFLECTIONS AFTER THE LEARNING

Reflecting on learning is an important step in metacognition. Encourage students to think about what they have learned by using some of these activities.

Wraparounds

1. Participants form a circle.

2. Each individual takes a turn telling . . .

   a. Something the student will use from information or activities learned today

   b. Something the student will remember from today

   c. A significant AHA! from this session

   d. I have learned _____

   e. I hope to learn _____

Talking Topic

1. Form A/B partners.

2. A tells a fact to B.

3. B gives another fact back.

4. Partners keep swapping facts back and forth.

Variation A

1. Each student writes two important things he or she has learned.

2. Form A/B partners. Name one A and the other one B.

3. A shares one thing he or she has learned.

4. B shares one thing he or she has learned.

5. A shares the other important item learned.

6. B shares the other important item learned.

Variation B

1. Form A/B partners.

2. A starts discussing a topic, concept, or standard being studied.

3. The teacher gives a signal, such as a hand clap.

4. B takes up with the discussion where A left off.

5. Clap again, and A continues the discussion.

6. Repeat as many times as necessary. Before the last turn, clap and say, "Now bring this to closure."

Conversation Circles

1. Form a conversation circle with a group of three students.

2. Ask students to assume A, B, or C names.

3. A starts talking and continues until given the signal to stop.

4. B continues with the topic.

5. C picks up the topic.

6. Continue until there are no more facts or ideas to add to the topic.

Donut

1. Draw a donut shape.

2. On the outside, write, "I am learning."

3. On the inside, write, "I know."

4. Ask students to share what they know about the topic. Write their responses on the donut.

Variation

1. Students form an inside and outside circle like a donut shape.

2. The students on the inside of the circle face the students on the outside.

3. Each student shares what he or she knows.

4. The inside circle moves clockwise, and the outside moves counterclockwise to continue sharing.

Rotation Reflection

1. Post charts around the room with a related topic written on each sheet.

2. Assign small groups to each location. Encourage groups to share ideas and views on the topic written on the chart.

3. Have a recorder fill in the chart with the great ideas generated.

4. Give a signal for the groups to stop talking. Ask the groups to move to the next chart and respond to that topic.

5. Groups continue around the room, visiting each chart in turn and adding ideas.

6. When all groups have visited all the charts, take time to review. At the chart they visit last, ask the group to consolidate the information and report it to the whole group.

Paper Pass

This activity uses several large pieces of chart paper.

1. Place a different subject heading at the top of each piece of chart paper.

2. Have each group brainstorm and write down what they know about the topic.

3. The group passes the paper to another group.

4. The second group reads all that has been written, then writes down what else they know about the topic.

5. The second group passes the paper to another group, who also adds to the sheet.

6. The process continues until all groups have contributed to all the subjects.

7. On the last pass, the group finds references for the statements on the chart paper.

8. Instruct students to place a page number and/or source beside each reference.

9. Share and post all the papers.

Draw It!

1. Each set of partners needs a large piece of poster paper and a marker.

2. Partners discuss and come to consensus on an important scene from the study.

3. After deciding, the first student starts the drawing.

4. The second student adds to the picture.

5. The partners swap the marker back and forth until the picture is complete.

6. Show students how to use the picture as a graphic organizer.

7. Instruct the students to brainstorm and write each fact learned about the topic around the picture.

8. Periodically during the study of the unit, have partners add more facts around the drawing.

9. Encourage students to use the drawing as a review before a test or an "open-picture" test.

More Ideas!

Select the items from the following list that are appropriate. Create a "Data Board," leaving room for feedback from the students in each section chosen. Students respond to the appropriate question, and their answers are posted. They can keep adding information to the board during the unit.

B   What I Brought

W   What I Want

L   Learnings for Me

S   Suggestions for Next Time

Q   Questions I Have

G   Guesses

P   Pluses

M   Minuses

I   Insights

R   Requests

F   Favorites

D   Dislikes

T   Teach Me!

- Journaling: Students need time allotted to write journal entries of their requests, comments, questions, and reflections
- Plotting data on a variety of graphic organizers
- Polls and interviews
- Conferences
- Performances
- Pre- and posttests
- Portfolios

Grand Finale Comment

Give students a task to do as they are leaving the class. This is the "Grand Finale Comment." These comments can give you feedback about student learning, the difficulties groups or individuals encountered, and students' feelings about the situations. Try some of the prompts listed below.

Individual

- Today I learned . . . Tomorrow I need . . .
- Today I felt . . . because . . .
- I would color today [name color] because . . .
- I hope we . . . next.
- One word to describe today is . . .
- I felt like a [name animal] during the . . . because . . .

Group

- Our group was great today when we . . .
- Tomorrow we are going to . . .
- A theme song for our work today would be . . .

ONGOING ASSESSMENT

In classrooms everywhere, teachers are using authentic strategies to teach the standards. They also use authentic tools to assess the standards, matching the learning to the assessment. For example, when students work on a project, they are assessed on their work throughout the development of the project as well as on their final report on the project.

Usually a rubric is developed and used throughout the entire process, so that the student, the parents, and the teacher understand the criteria and expectations and can assess progress along the way.

Portfolios also are now used in many classes, with teachers relating that the portfolios are being used as vehicles for reflection, ongoing conversations, and goal setting between and among students, teachers, and parents.

PORTFOLIOS

What Are They?

Portfolios are collections of student work for specific purposes based on criteria that support and provide evidence of application and understanding of the targeted concepts or skills. Portfolios can identify progress, show evidence of success, support evaluation and grading, and contain pieces that show what additional learning needs to take place. They are a way of facilitating ongoing feedback and reflection during the learning process.

Why Do We Use Them?

Richard Stiggins (1993) suggests that a portfolio is like a color video with sound, much more vivid than just a test paper. It gives a much fuller picture and provides supportive evidence to substantiate the feedback or grade that has been given. It also encourages student ownership and reflection on progress toward learning goals. Portfolios contain evidence of growth, with initial samples of work and pieces added periodically to show progress. Part of the portfolio process is the ongoing dialogue about quality and criteria that occurs between and among the teacher, students, and peers. This enables students to reflect on their work and to analyze quality and set goals.

How Do We Use Them?

Often, the portfolio is a partnership, with both the teacher and student being involved in selecting pieces to put in the portfolio. The teacher will set criteria for selection and allow several choices to be made by the students. Some teachers use colored dots to identify pieces that are included: red dot on student-selected pieces, yellow dot on teacher-selected pieces, and green dot on teacher/student-selected pieces. There can be four steps in the portfolio process: Collect, Select, Reflect, and Project (Burke, Fogarty, & Belgrad, 1994).

Collect

Pieces are gathered from the beginning of the year or unit based on criteria. They may include homework, projects, written pieces, mind maps, tests, assignments, cassettes or videos, letters, graphic organizers, lab reports, poems, raps, audiotapes, and book reviews.

Evidence in the portfolio may be varied depending on the subject area.

> Portfolios tell a story . . . put in anything that helps tell the story. (Paulson, Paulson, & Meyer, 1991, p. 1)

Select

Students select pieces based on guidelines. The criteria may include

- Best piece/something I'm proud of
- Work in progress
- Student/teacher selection
- Most improved/difficult piece
- Special or free choice

Every so often, students will examine the pieces and decide which items should stay in the collection and which should be deleted. Pieces may be deleted because

- There is enough evidence of that competency already.
- It doesn't really show what is needed.
- A new piece is superior.

Reflect

The student will then write a reflection to be attached to the piece that explains why it was selected and what criteria it satisfies. Over time, students add other pieces that may show growth from the last item or can replace others. Not all pieces are necessarily the best effort, but may be included as baseline evidence to show growth in the future.

Project

Reflections and examination of items can lead to goal setting. Students can decide what to do next, what to focus on, what needs improvement, and what to celebrate.

Portfolio conferences are effective ways to share student growth with others. Students articulate their learning and goal setting to colleagues, parents, and significant others.

Each student is an individual, and each portfolio will be unique to each learner, showing the individuality and growth of the learner.

GRADING

Teachers tend to give grades for many different reasons. There seems to be no commonly accepted yardstick for student achievement. Opinions about what should be evaluated and what actually is evaluated are aspects of continuing dialogue among educators. Grades are often given to

1. Measure content mastery—to show what the student knows in the subject area

2. Chart progress—to communicate progress on individual goals and show the working level on a specific content

3. Motivate students—to prod the student to work harder or to reward the student for trying and giving so much effort

4. Provide information to a variety of audiences—students turn in their grades for recognition, awards, scholarships, and admittance into colleges and universities

Grades are not the only tools teachers use for their final evaluation of what students have learned. Ongoing assessments have been giving feedback throughout the unit of study, and there are several possible class scenarios for the final evaluation:

- Give the common posttest to compare the pre- and postperformances. This is the same test given as the pre-assessment. The comparison of pre- and posttests may show progress or competence or lack of progress. If skills or content require more practice, the teacher will need to plan for that to happen. The results could also show areas of weakness for further study. Posttests will determine whether students are knowledgeable, have improved, and have enduring understanding or need further practice for mastery to be acquired.

- Develop a test that evaluates the material studied by the different groups in the adjusted assignments. This test is based on the level of complexity of the study. Some of the questions would be on all tests. These questions would come from the information presented to the total group throughout the study. With this instrument, the groups of students would be given a written test consisting of the material the individual groups had studied. This system allows teachers to communicate students' achievements on the specific information that they have been studying. They are not being compared with the students working on a less challenging or more difficult area of the study.

- Some evaluation instruments combine both scenarios. There are questions given to all the students, and then a portion of the test is developed specifically to address an individual student or group of students. All the above scenarios are examples of written tests given at the end of a section of study. They may not stand alone as a final grade. The written test grade may be only one piece of the data that compile the final grade. Evidence and grades have been gathered throughout to show a true picture of the student's performance.

AUTHENTIC TASKS

An *authentic task* asks students to perform tasks in a realistic, real-world context (Wiggins & McTighe, 1998). This may be part of an instructional activity, such as a demonstration, a presentation, or a role-playing event. The students are asked to demonstrate mastery in ways that are of interest to them. Therefore the knowledge is shown or demonstrated in a way the student can convey it best.

Assessments for Authentic Performances

Examples of assessment tools include rubrics, anecdotal notes, checklists, journal entries, samples of student work, self-evaluation, and conferences. These tools would be used to assess various types of learning activities, from role-playing to projects. Learning needs to be the goal, but making the appropriate grade is often the main focus. Conveying an accurate portrait of students as learners is a complex task.

For example, students are asked to work a problem in math. Then they might be asked to draw the problem and then explain the problem to someone else. In reading, students might be asked to read about a character at a certain point in the text. Then they might be asked to draw the character and put the character in the setting described in the text. Another time, they could be asked to role-play that character or find the background music to depict the character's feelings during a particular part of the story.

These are authentic strategies that allow the learner to interpret meaning. Some of these could be assessed with a written form, but most would need an authentic assessment tool to match the authentic task. Figure 18 lists tasks and products that teachers can use to assess student learning in more authentic ways.

Clear expectations and criteria need to be communicated up front so that students know the target and work toward it.

Figure 18. Performance Assessment Examples

Verbal/ Linguistic	Visual/ Spatial	Bodily/ Kinesthetic	Musical/ Rhythmic	Logical/ Mathematical
Plan a trip. Conduct a panel. Create a talk show. Teach a lesson. Complete a portfolio. Conduct a survey. Write an editorial.	Make a mural. Create a brochure. Create a costume. Design a PowerPoint. Draw an illustration.	Conduct a demonstration. Develop a role-play. Create a puppet play. Demonstrate an experiment.	Choreograph a dance. Write lyrics to a song. Create a poem. Write a rap. Create a cheer. Create a CD with theme songs.	Create a flow chart. Create a time line. Show step-by-step process. Sequence of events. Write a "how-to" manual.

For a more accurate report, a teacher includes a grade, a portfolio to show the evidence to support the grade, a comment section with specific data about individual performance, and a parent conference for students and teachers to discuss areas of needs and areas of mastery.

Student Choices

Teachers are experimenting with a variety of ways to allow students to show what they know. One teacher has been quite creative in designing tests. She offered the students two options. The first option was traditional, consisting of 20 right and wrong answers to volume and area problems, with memorized formulas and no calculator. Points were given for correct formula, answer, and label of answer. The second option allowed calculator use and a formula sheet for students during the test. The problems were applications to real life, thus not perfect math numbers. The shapes were real ice cream cones or lawn sprinklers and showed the actual uses of formulas in our everyday lives.

The second option involved in-depth thinking and multiple-step problems, and it allowed some room for alternate answers. The teacher reported that several students were quite excited about having a choice. Several were hesitant, not knowing which was the best test for them to show what they knew. Several had difficulty figuring out why the teacher might give partial credit for a wrong answer.

FINAL GRADES

Many agendas influence the final grade. Some capable students do not work very hard but still receive an A. Other students apply themselves and work diligently to do their best but still do not get an A. Grades can motivate as well as show evidence of performance and acquired knowledge, but they also can be demoralizing. Comments need to be made that clarify the effort or lack of effort made by each student. When making written comments, write specific observable statements, omitting adjectives and adverbs. Just the facts! Adjectives and adverbs make the comments judgmental. Write down what you have observed in order to find patterns of behaviors, strengths, and weaknesses. This identifies specific needs for planning strategically. A strong work ethic is one of the competencies listed under "Self-Motivation" in Goleman's (1995) *Emotional Intelligences*. Teachers need to honor persistence, tenacity, and effort.

Tomlinson (2001) suggests that some teachers give students grades based on their success on the material they were studying. An identifying code can tell the parent that this grade was given at the student's level to show competency, not for comparison with the rest of the class. Thus a student might get an A working at his or her own level but a D in comparison with classmates.

As we move to a more differentiated classroom, we need to communicate with parents, students, and the broader community so that they understand our intentions and the changes that are taking place. When they comprehend, they will support the processes that are best for students.

As learning tasks need to be differentiated, so do assessment strategies, so that all learners get to learn in a variety of ways and show what they know in ways that are comfortable, durable, and "suit" the learner.

1. How do you currently pre-assess students?

2. How are you meeting the affective needs of your students? How do you incorporate the interests of your students into the learning experience? How do you combine these with prior knowledge and skills?

3. What data are you presently using to plan the instructional and assessment process?

4. What are you going to do first to improve assessment and feedback in your classroom?

WHEN WE DESIGN CLOTHES FOR PEOPLE, WE CONSIDER THEIR height, weight, and shape because those things influence the size of the clothing. As we know, not every student wears the same size, and of course we don't force them into a size small when they need a large. Not every student has the same background and experience, and so is not necessarily as knowledgeable or skillful in every topic or skill as other students. We also know that we may get tired of wearing the same old thing, and students get tired of the same old thing in the classroom, too. Yet we often force them to endure the same lesson (in the same format) whether they already know the content or haven't any idea what is going on. This is why adjustments need to be made in their learning.

ADJUSTABLE ASSIGNMENTS

What Are They?

In classrooms everywhere, we are examining how we can get a better fit for all students. *Adjustable assignments* allow teachers to help students focus on essential skills and understanding key concepts, recognizing that they may be at different levels of readiness. Some may or may not be able to handle different levels of complexity or abstraction. Although the assignment is adjusted for different groups of learners, the standards, concepts, and content of each assignment have the same focus and each student has the opportunity to develop essential skills and understanding at his or her appropriate level of challenge. The activities better ensure that students explore ideas at their levels, while building on prior knowledge and experiencing incremental growth.

Why Do We Use Them?

Using adjusted assignments allows students to begin learning where they are and to work on challenging and worthwhile tasks. If we were growing flowers and some of the seeds had sprouted and were ready to flower, we would not pull them out by the roots and make them start again from seed. It sounds a bit bizarre when we think about it. We, of course, would give the plants that were advanced in their growth the light, water, and food they needed and would nurture the seedlings that were just sprouting to help them bloom and grow. Adjusting assignments allows for reinforcement or extension of concepts based on student readiness, learning styles, and/or multiple intelligence preferences. Appropriate adjustments in the learning have a greater chance of providing a "flow" experience in which each student is presented with challenging work that just exceeds his or her skill level.

This also increases the chances of success for each learner because that success is within reach, and ultimately success will be highly motivating. Adjusting assignments also decreases the chances of "downshifting" and the sense of helplessness that students feel when a challenge is beyond their capabilities.

How Do We Use Them?

Initially, as in any planning process, the concepts, skills, and content that will be the focus of the activity are identified and aligned with targeted standards and expectations.

Using some method of pre-assessment (quizzes, journal entries, class discussions and data collection techniques, learning profiles, etc.), teachers gather data to determine the prior knowledge of students for the new content or the skill that is targeted for learning. The pre-assessment data are compiled. Then the key standards and concepts to be taught during the unit are determined. The teacher then decides which parts of the study should be taught to the total class and how they will be presented. The appropriate places to teach these concepts and/or skills are determined. Then comes the time to make decisions about any adjustable assignment. Assignments are adjusted to meet the needs of learners based on their present knowledge or skill levels. The following are questions the teacher will answer when making decisions about these assignments:

- What content does each group already know?
- What does each group need to learn?
- What strategies should be used to facilitate the learning of each portion?
- What is the most effective way to group students for each activity?
- What assessment tools will be used so that students will be accountable?
- Are the plans meeting the individual needs of the students?

Basic knowledge and experience vary among learners, so adjustable assignments may be needed. Here is an example that is typical of what teachers face every time they start planning for all of their students.

Example: Adjustable Assignments for Early Elementary Grades
The Money Unit

Figure 19, Part A, shows what the groups of students know and can do based on the pre-assessment data analysis. This does not show numbers in the group, but the knowledge or

---

Figure 19. Adjustable-Assignments Model: Money

Figure Key:
A. What do they know at the beginning of the study?
B. What do they need to learn next?

	High Degree of Mastery	Approaching Mastery	Beginning Mastery
B	Bring in the dollar bills to make change. Make more combinations of money. When given a price, can pay and/or get accurate change.	How to count the coins with mixed values. How to give and count change.	Use patterns with coins. Fit pattern to correct coin. Fit value of each coin. Order of the coins according to worth.
A	Identifies coins. Knows all the patterns. Adds up coins. Gives or counts change. Uses coins as a consumer.	Identifies coins. Knows 1, 5, 10 patterns. Fits value with each coin. Can order the coins according to worth. Uses patterns with the correct coins.	Knows 1, 5, 10 patterns. Realizes use of money to buy things. Recognizes some coins.

Standard: To be able to use currency in daily situations
Content: Coins
Pre-assessment tool to determine students' knowledge base: A teacher-made manipulation test

---

skill the group has. Part B is completed with tasks, assignments, or lessons that students require to continue their learning and understanding.

Part A: High Degree of Mastery. What does this group know at the beginning of the study? Students know the names of the coins. They can count their money and make accurate change. They are consumer-wise as far as using money to purchase goods. Some of these students have been shopping in the neighborhood stores. Therefore they have the background knowledge base. Other students will need those basics before they can proceed. Real-life experiences have taught the content. Therefore these students need to work with elements of money other than the basics.

Part A: Approaching Mastery. What does this group know at the beginning of the study? These students have shown that they know the names of the coins. They are limited as far as the other concepts being taught. Therefore they need to begin counting and adding up coins and working with different combinations of money. As they advance, they can move to purchasing and receiving or giving change.

Part A: Beginning Mastery. What does this group know at the beginning of the study? This group of students shows that they know few if any of the names of the coins or their worth. They will need all the information taught so that they develop a knowledge base. Because of adjustable assignments, all these groups will be challenged and will learn information using a variety of strategies based on their needs. The students will work in groups that are designed to meet their needs. There will be ongoing assessment throughout the learning to provide appropriate feedback and to adjust assignments further.

Part B: Beginning Mastery. What do they need to learn next? From pre-assessment data, the teacher will be able to identify those students who have gaps in their previous learning or little background in the new area of study. Without filling in the gaps, the students will not be able to learn new information. During the study of the topic, allowances are made to work with these students where they are. The beginning group needs to learn the patterns that go with the different coins. For example, the students can count by fives but do not realize the same pattern applies to the nickel. In addition, the order of the coins by value needs to be learned. Many times, when children who are shown a nickel and a dime are asked, "Which is worth more?" many will choose the nickel because it is larger in size. This has to be taught to be able to give and get change.

Part B: Approaching Mastery. What do they need to learn next? After a strong pre-assessment, the teacher may find there is a group of students who are ready for the standard content to be taught. Next they need to learn how to count the coins with mixed values and how to give and count change.

Part B: High Degree of Mastery. What do they need to learn next? When the pre-assessment data are compiled, there may be a group of students who know the content and will be bored if they have to go over all of it again. Although they know the content, they can always go deeper or be more analytical, creative, or practical with it. This group of students needs to explore different ways we are consumers. They also need to learn how to use more combinations of money, pay and get accurate change, and use dollar bills.

As a result of the information gathered during pre-assessment, the teacher designed three meaningful activities at the levels the three groups needed.

The more advanced group (a high degree of mastery) worked at running a snack shop for recess and lunch. They priced the snacks and sold them, making change and counting the cash to calculate their earnings. They also used calculators to check their work.

During class time, these students engaged in activities that led them further in their understanding of coins and their relationships to each other. Using actual coins at a center, the students challenged one another with combinations. "I have ten coins that make a dollar," said Pat. "That's ten dimes," chimed in Tara. "I have six coins that make a dollar," said Corey. "That could be three quarters, two dimes, and a nickel," said Jodie. The game became quite competitive as pairs kept score of their successes.

Students also used calculators to total amounts of items on their wish lists for birthday gifts.

The group of students who were able to recognize the coins (approaching mastery) used coin stamps to make patterns with their partners. They challenged other group members to identify coins and give the total. They collected discarded toys and items from home and priced them to create a class garage sale. They priced the items and had a garage sale using money.

The group of students who needed more experience (the beginners) to recognize the coins played a coin game similar to "Concentration," in which they had to be able to recognize the coins and match them. They also began to match equivalents, such as five pennies and a nickel equaling a dime, two nickels equaling a dime, and so on.

All students were able to shop at the snack shop and garage sale and practiced using coins appropriately. They also were integrated into the operation of the two sales and worked with more experienced students who modeled and added to their learning.

All students were engaged in interesting and challenging activities that added to their experience.

Figure 20 shows what the data might look like for a Spanish standard of everyday conversation and the topic of giving directions.

Figure 20.   Adjustable Assignments: Spanish

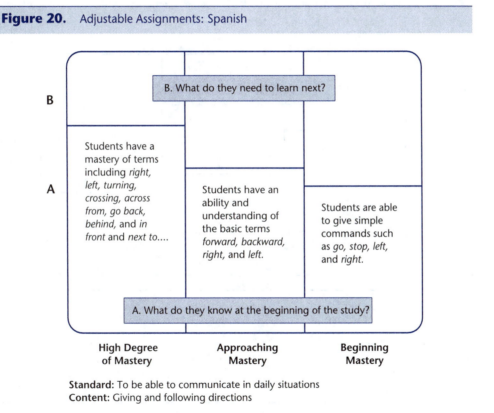

B. What do they need to learn next?

B

A

Students have a mastery of terms including *right, left, turning, crossing, across from, go back, behind,* and *in front* and *next to....*

Students have an ability and understanding of the basic terms *forward, backward, right,* and *left.*

Students are able to give simple commands such as *go, stop, left,* and *right.*

A. What do they know at the beginning of the study?

| High Degree of Mastery | Approaching Mastery | Beginning Mastery |

Standard: To be able to communicate in daily situations
Content: Giving and following directions

Section A shows what the three groups of students know and are able to do in relation to the standard and content. Section B would show what needs to be done to extend the learning for that group.

The **Advanced Mastery** group (only four students) went online and found street maps of Mexico City. They wrote directions to areas or points of interest and produced posters advertising the attributes of that location.

The **Approaching Mastery** group designed a board game that used the vocabulary of giving directions. They produced interesting adaptations of board games with which they were familiar and wrote task cards for the games using vocabulary beyond what they had used in the past, incorporating new terminology.

The **Beginners** group worked in pairs to give one another directions to various areas in the school. They drew task cards and were able to direct one another to the cafeteria, office, or computer lab using Spanish. They then participated in a game similar to Twister, in which they spun a wheel and followed the directions given.

More levels of readiness may be identified and adjusted if needed, but when first beginning this process, three levels may be complicated enough for the teacher to manage.

After the pre-assessment has been given, the teacher analyzes the data and plots them on the chart in Section A (see Figure 21).

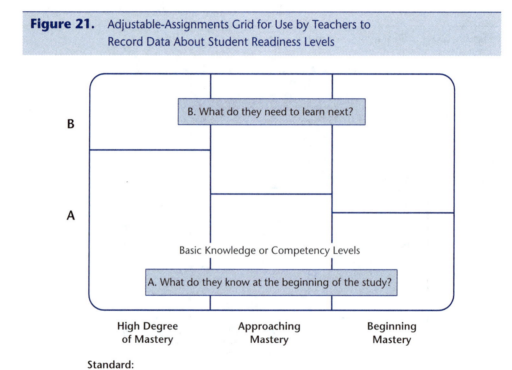

Figure 21.   Adjustable-Assignments Grid for Use by Teachers to Record Data About Student Readiness Levels

B. What do they need to learn next?

B

A

Basic Knowledge or Competency Levels

A. What do they know at the beginning of the study?

High Degree of Mastery   **Approaching Mastery**   **Beginning Mastery**

Standard:
Content:

Note: This is not about number or time

After the data have been entered, the teacher needs to consider what the students still need to know and be able to do to extend their learning. Teachers then fill in Part B of the grid with a learning that is suitably challenging and engaging in order to bring those learners to the next level. It may be a lesson, activity, task, or assignment. There may be different assignments that students do independently and that are given at two levels, in pairs, or in small groups, thus leaving the teacher free to interact and facilitate new content or processes with another group of students. The teacher may choose from a variety of curriculum approaches, such as projects, centers, integration, or problem-based learning.

CURRICULUM COMPACTING

What Is It?

Curriculum compacting is a strategy first shared by Joe Renzulli (see Reis & Renzulli, 1992) of the University of Connecticut (see also Tomlinson, 1999, 2001). It provides for the student who is very capable and knowledgeable in a particular topic in a subject area. It is a way of maximizing time for the more advanced learner.

Why Do We Use It?

Many students, because of prior experience, interests, and opportunities, may bring to the topic prior knowledge and skills that have been acquired over time. These may have been acquired through voracious reading, travel, and personal interest about a topic or from a mentor or role model who has had an influence on the learner. It is for these students that compacting may be used on occasion in order to enrich their curricula, enhance and stretch their thinking, and help them develop into more self-directed learners. In many classrooms, where teaching to the middle is the norm, some learners are bored as they "repeat history," and others are lost because they don't have the background or experience they need to understand or be able to do what is expected of them. Compacting/enriching (see Figure 22) may be used with high-end or advanced learners identified after a pre-assessment is given. It is important to allow all learners to move at their own pace, thus creating the "relaxed alertness" that Kohn (as cited in Caine & Caine, 1997) suggests. Challenging experiences that are perceived as "doable" in a learning situation put students into a state of "flow," thus engaging them at their levels of challenge and not frustrating or boring them by giving them too difficult or too easy a task.

How Do We Do It?

Phase 1

In this phase, after an exploratory session in which students are able to access prior knowledge and discuss their initial concepts and knowledge, a pre-assessment is given.

This may be in the form of

- A pretest
- A conference where the learner shares knowledge and understanding about the topic
- A portfolio presentation in which students show evidence of their comprehension and skill levels (any or all of these may be used)

Phase 2

After the pre-assessment, the teacher analyzes the data and identifies what the student already knows and has mastered and what the student still needs to learn.

This additional knowledge or skill may be acquired by

- Joining the total class group for that concept or information
- Independent study
- Homework assignments

Figure 22.   Curriculum Compacting: Used to Provide Enrichment
for Advanced Learners Beyond the Regular Curriculum

Phase 1	Phase 2 Analyze data	Phase 3
Exploratory Phase	Mastery: skills, concepts What have they mastered?	Advanced Level Challenges
Pre-Assessment: • Test • Conference • Portfolio conference	Needs to Master: What else do they need to know?	• Investigation • Problem-Based Learning • Service Learning • Project • Contract
To Find Out What the Learner • Knows • Needs to know • Wants to know	How Will They Learn It? • Gain with whole class • Independent study • Homework • Mentor/buddy in or out of school • On-line learning	Opportunities for Successful Intelligence Sternberg, 1996 • Analytical • Practical • Creative Assessment

- Collaborating with a mentor or learning buddy in or outside school
- Online learning

Phase 3

Once the missing pieces have been added, the students may choose or be offered

- An investigation or research project
- An ill-structured problem to solve
- A service-learning opportunity
- A project
- A negotiated contract
- A special assignment

These assignments facilitate the challenge of applying their knowledge and skill in a practical and/or creative way. Robert Sternberg (1996), a noted psychologist, has defined *successful intelligence* as including the aspects of being analytical, practical, and creative, not just knowing.

This allows learners to enhance their understanding and also obtain an added perspective on the subject matter. Compacting/enrichment is a strategy often used with academically gifted or talented students to enhance their curricula. It may be done as a pullout or partial-pullout model or orchestrated in the classroom with the subject teacher. If students are pulled out, they should not miss other subject areas of study that they have not mastered. Teachers must be sure that students really do have full mastery of the concept, not just surface-level knowledge. Students should not be required to complete the regular classroom assignments in the subject for which they have compacted out.

What Does It Look Like?

Some forms of compacting/enrichment take into consideration that some students have ample prior knowledge or experience to warrant a full semester or grade-level subject advancement. This would include the French student skipping first-year French because she is fluent in the language. Another example is a pre-algebra student skipping Algebra 1 and starting in Algebra 2. Another scenario is the first grader going up to the third grade for reading each day.

Compacting/enrichment also occurs when students in several grade-level math classes are identified as being beyond curriculum expectations and so are pulled out of the classes during math time for enhanced or accelerated learning with an identified extension teacher.

Collaborative Planning Models

In some schools, there are several teachers teaching the same grade level (such as four teachers teaching third grade). Teachers in each class pre-assess the students in a math concept and cluster them by skill level into four new class groupings of advanced, competent, basic, and beginning (see Figure 23). The four teachers collaborate to design learning experiences for each group. Each of the four teachers takes one of the groups during math time and facilitates the learning for that particular group. This scenario encourages teacher collaboration to enhance the school's professional learning community. Teachers share resources, ideas, and strategies and further develop their repertoires of teaching through professional dialogue and problem solving. Common planning time may help facilitate this process. This could be used occasionally for special topics, and other math topics could be taught in the regular classroom. Each group may go into greater depth on a particular topic of interest and still reach the same goals.

In-Class Compacting/Enrichment

As shown in Figure 24, any class may divide into a number of groupings in relationship to mastery. There may be one or two, a few, or no students who need to have enrichment offered because of a high level of mastery. The number of students in each group may vary depending on their skill levels in relationship to the standards.

We are not suggesting that you track students or restrict them to homogeneous groups such as the bluebirds, buzzards, and crows for any length of time. But sometimes skill development is needed at a challenging but not overwhelming level. This could be done occasionally to deepen skill levels and help all learners, beginning with where they are in relation to the targeted standard. Sometimes a small, homogeneous group will help students "drill deeply" with a skill, but more often, heterogeneous groups will be more helpful and allow students to "cross-pollinate" with a variety of fertile ideas.

Figure 23.   Collaborative Jigsaw Compacting

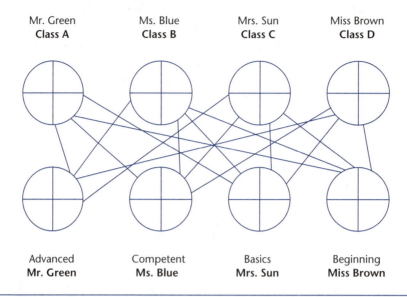

Figure 24.   In-Class Compacting

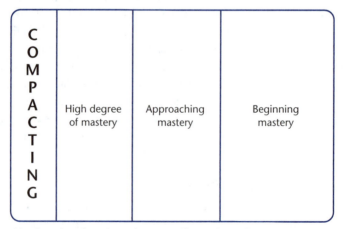

Number of students in each group will vary depending on the topic or standard.

Curriculum compacting may be used for very advanced student(s). Often compacting is not required.

Students may work alone, with a partner with similar interests, or in a small group of students focusing on the same materials and/or applications. This would depend on the number of students and their interests and learning profiles.

Agendas

The teacher may want to have students develop an *agenda* to keep track of time and tasks (see Figure 25). Students fill in the date and the task column of the agenda for the class, day, or unit of study. After each task is completed, they detail the progress in the log column and then chronicle their reflections in the next column. Each student and the teacher then conference and sign off in the last column.

Students may use double-duty logs (see Figure 26) to monitor steps and record reflections as they work on the assignment. This ongoing assessment helps both teacher and students clearly see the successes, progress, and needs throughout the assignment. It helps the students keep track of their time, reflect on their work, and set goals for the next step.

Adjusting and compacting are two techniques that strategic teachers use to help students feel comfortable and capable in their learning. Most instructional strategies can be used to adjust the learning.

Figure 25.   Personal Agenda to Keep Track of Time and Tasks

✿ ✿ ✿   A Personal Agenda   ✿ ✿ ✿

My Agenda (name):   _____

Beginning on (date):   _____

Dates	Student Tasks	Log— How I Used My Time	Reflections	Completion Date— Teacher & Student Sign-Off

Figure 26. Double-Duty Log

Double-duty logs allow students to record or list facts and information about content or process and then reflect on that information immediately or at another time to integrate it into their thinking and deepen their understanding. It allows students to process the information and make sense or meaning. It also facilitates revisiting the material to clarify or add to the thinking.

Facts or Ideas	Thoughts and Reflections

FLEXIBLE GROUPING

Finding the Right Size

Flexible grouping is often needed to facilitate differentiated instruction. Everyone has strong and weak areas of ability and interest. Students need to be placed in groups that maximize their instructional time based on their performance levels. Grouping flexibility allows students to move according to their demonstrated performance, interests, and varied knowledge base levels. Students are grouped to meet their instructional, emotional, and personal needs. If a group of students get along socially, they will usually meet the instructional expectations.

By remembering to use each component of TAPS (total, alone, partner, small group) in planning, the individual social needs have a greater chance of being met. These grouping methods can be used where they fit in the classroom. Some students can work well in all of these ways, but every learner has preferences (Goleman, 1995).

A person who is very strong in his or her intrapersonal intelligence processes may prefer to solve problems better by working alone. He or she is able to solve the problem independently and does not see the need to work with a group. It takes time to think. Often this student will get really quiet in a group situation and become more metacognitive in order to process the learning.

Other students will be very strong in interpersonal intelligence. They are sometimes called "social butterflies." They feel the need to talk about concepts to understand them fully. They prefer to work with others rather than alone. These students bring empathy and harmony to the group.

Groups need

- Ample space to work
- Clear directions and procedures
- Rules and guidelines established
- Individual roles assigned for group responsibilities
- A time frame assigned for on-task work
- To tap into all members' strengths

Some students learn best while working alone; some work better when grouped with others. This offers students options designed to tap into different readiness levels, interests, talents, and learning modalities. An effective, quality pre-assessment helps decide which type of grouping will be the most effective for that particular part of the learning. Flexible grouping is in constant use and is forever changing in planning differentiated instruction.

Total Group

Alone

Partner

Small Group

TAPS (a rap)

Remember!

Some things need to be taught to the class as a whole.
There are certain things the Total Group should be told.

Working Alone, students get to problem solve in their own way.
They will be in charge of what they think, do, and say.

With a Partner, many thoughts and ideas they can share.
They can work and show each other the solutions there.

Effective Small Groups work together to cooperate.
Using the group's ideas and talents, their learning will accelerate.

So use a variety of ways to group students you see.
This TAPS into students' potential, as it should be.

GROUPING STRATEGIES

The following are some ways to group students to better meet their learning needs.

Knowledge of a Subject

Cluster grouping of a small number of students within a heterogeneously grouped classroom can be used. This way, the students are grouped according to their prior experiences and knowledge about the topic. A pre-assessment is given to determine what the students know at the beginning of the study. This allows each group to be given tasks that involve a variety of opportunities for novices as well as experienced students. When grouped in this manner, students are challenged and are interested in the work rather than being bored by information they already have received or frustrated by something they know nothing about.

For instance, in a science curriculum, one or more students might be very knowledgeable about the unit on creatures of the sea. These students are a valuable resource to the entire class in this area of high interest. They need to study and add to their knowledge base rather than review the information they already know. The next unit studied in the science class might be something that is unfamiliar to them, so they would need to acquire the basics and move in with a different group to study. The knowledge base of an individual is based on experiences. The novice or beginner needs more of the basic topic information than the experienced learner does.

Ability to Perform a Task or a Skill

All people have certain talents and skills that they can perform better than others. One type of group to form would be the very skilled. Another might be those who are less skilled in a given area and need lots of help.

Still another would be forming teams of masters, those who do the subject well, and of apprentices, those who need one-on-one direction and assistance.

The purpose of *ability grouping* is for the student to work with materials and information that are challenging and stimulating at a personal level. Assignments differ by making adjustments consisting of varying levels of difficulty. Questions are molded to pull information from students according to what they can comprehend. This fosters continued growth because one size does not fit all.

Interests in a Specific Area of the Content

If a learner is interested in a topic or subject, the desire and emotions involved engage the learner. Conversations, interest surveys, and inventories give teachers information to weave into the learning. Why? By addressing what the learner is interested in, teachers have a link for the new learning. The desire to learn more is there. Students are interested in the arts, sports, games, role models, and outside activities that challenge their minds. In school, if their interests can be found, they are more likely to be engaged. Learning comes easier, and attention spans are longer for content that students are interested in learning.

Peer-to-Peer Tutoring

Having students assist each other with specific needs is a way to give them responsibility for understanding what they know and how they can use the information. The student who is tutoring is gaining from this experience. If you teach something, you remember it and realize what you know and how you know it. The learner is gaining from the experience, too, because it is an individualized instruction that is tailored to a personal need. Students often communicate with each other using different words than the teacher would, and sometimes their ways of explaining information may be easier for the peer to understand. Some examples are peer tutoring, peer reading, and peer journaling.

A good time to use peer-to-peer tutoring is when a student has just caught on to a process, skill, concept, or standard. When the "lightbulb" goes on, learners want to tell others how they solved it or the details of their understanding. For example, a student has been struggling and working to understand a concept. She finally understands and "gets it." The learner is ready to tell everyone how this happened. She will give the step-by-step thinking process and explain it in language for others to understand. It is that "Finally I got it" feeling. There is a desire to say, "Let me tell you all about it!"

Automaticity happens through repetitive practice, and actions become hardwired in procedural memory in the cerebellum. This is the expert. It is a high-level thinking process to break down a procedure into clearly articulated steps. This reinforces the procedure in both the capable student and the novice.

Cooperative Learning

Productive and flexible partner and group work are essential in a differentiated classroom. Remember, if the people in a group get along socially, they will usually get the job done! Students learn social skills as well as cognitive skills and most often use higher levels of thinking as they discuss and clarify information. When using cooperative learning, the group comes to a consensus on a common goal or a specific assignment. Those in the group are assigned specific roles to play for a particular task. Both individual and group accountability are built in as an important part of a cooperative learning experience. Experts in cooperative group learning recommend that groups be structured heterogeneously:

> Of great importance to this discussion are the Lou and others (1996) findings that students of all ability levels benefit from ability grouping when compared with not grouping at all—students of low ability actually perform worse when they are placed [in] homogeneous groups with students of low ability—as opposed to students of low ability placed in heterogeneous groups. (Marzano, Pickering, & Pollack, 2001, p. 87)

For heterogeneous groupings that occur randomly, try using the grid called "Stick Picks" (see Figure 27), based on an idea shared by public school teacher W. Brenner (Fremont, CA).

Figure 27. Stick Picks: Used to Create Random Groups of Heterogeneous Learners

By using sticks you can efficiently and quickly create random groups. As students enter the class, hand each one a stick. The following list shows you the colors to put on each stick. Number the sticks and use magic marker to put the two colors on the stick. You can use craft sticks or tongue depressors. After you group the students, collect the sticks so that they are not lost or destroyed.

Number	Color	Color	Number	Color	Color
1	blue	orange	19	yellow	orange
2	yellow	pink	20	green	purple
3	red	purple	21	red	pink
4	green	pink	22	blue	purple
5	yellow	orange	23	green	orange
6	blue	purple	24	yellow	pink
7	green	purple	25	blue	pink
8	red	pink	26	green	purple
9	red	orange	27	red	orange
10	green	orange	28	yellow	orange
11	blue	pink	29	yellow	pink
12	yellow	purple	30	green	purple
13	yellow	purple	31	blue	orange
14	red	orange	32	red	pink
15	green	pink	33	red	purple
16	blue	pink	34	yellow	purple
17	blue	purple	35	blue	pink
18	red	orange	36	green	orange

Every group of 4 sticks (1–4, 5–8, etc.) has all four colors: green, yellow, blue, and red, one on each stick. If that group of 4 is a team, then the teacher can assign the roles based on the four colors green, yellow, blue, and red. Random groups can be formed by partnering students with the same two colors. Some groups will have 2 students, some 3, and some 4.

To get 4 larger groups, use the colors yellow, green, red, and blue as group identifiers.
To form 3 large groups, use the colors orange, pink, and purple.
To get partners: 1 and 2 are a pair, 3 and 4, 5 and 6, and so on.

More Heterogeneous Groupings

Differentiated instruction accommodates academic diversity and heterogeneous grouping. "Wagon Wheel Teaming," based on an idea developed by Sheila Silversides (in Kagan, 1992), can be used to group students quickly and randomly into groups of three or four that include a beginning-level student, two average-level students, and an expert-level student. As shown in Figure 28, four concentric circles are fastened in the center with a paper fastener so that they can rotate. Students' names are recorded inside the four circles based on readiness or capability relating to a particular skill or concept. Or student names can be assigned to a circle based on learning styles, multiple intelligences, or reading levels to encourage true diversity and heterogeneous groupings. To form a new student group, keep the center circle stationary, move the next wheel one turn, the following wheel two turns, and the outer wheel three turns. Then you will have totally new groups of four from the center to the outer edge, with all three types of learners in each new group.

Sharing Groups

Sometimes, teachers group students to share information, to research a topic, or for review purposes. Students can learn so much from each other. It can be very refreshing for students to hear information from many sources, in many voices. It also facilitates the opportunity for review and processing to reinforce and clarify ideas. It can provide movement that is important to the physical needs of some learners.

Sharing can be done with students standing, sitting on the floor, sitting around a table, rearranging desks, or creating other comfortable spaces conducive to conversations. Plot these throughout the curriculum for conversations, discussions, and teaching that make the students responsible for their learning. This gives ownership!

Energizing Partners

Establish *energizing partners* for oral sharing and processing with a partner. Let students choose a classmate with whom they feel they can communicate effectively. For minimal

Figure 28. Wagon Wheel Teaming: Rotating Concentric Circles to Form Teams of Three or Four Learners at Different Levels

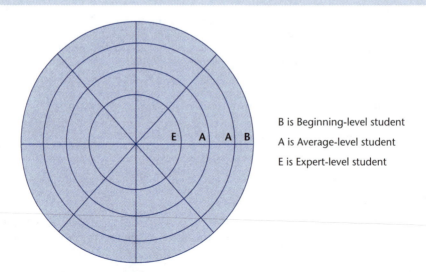

B is Beginning-level student

A is Average-level student

E is Expert-level student

movement, encourage students to choose a partner near where they sit. The partners leave their desks and stand and face each other to share information. Each set of partners decides who is Partner A; the other is Partner B. This helps equalize talking time. The teacher assigns the task and assigns Partners A and B roles and tasks. For example, the teacher says, "Go stand and face your partner. Partner A, you share what you remember we discussed from yesterday. Now Partner B, you share what you remember from yesterday's learning." The established duo can remain partners for a length of time. Some suggested times are a grading period, a semester, or during a particular unit of study. The reason they remain partners this long is so that the partners bond. They build trust and friendships and share information with more enthusiasm. However, in a differentiated environment, flexible grouping is ongoing, and all students need to and will work with all students at some point in time for a particular reason. This gives students a time to get out of their seats as well as to discuss the important parts of the learning. Instead of having just one student answer questions, half of the class is engaged in the learning at any given time.

Brainstorming Bash

Students form small groups and brainstorm ideas, thoughts, and solutions. After posing the task, give each group member time to answer and process the answer on his or her own. This think time gives each person personal information to share with the group.

Have a recorder in each group write down all the thoughts that are shared. This way, the group follows the conversation auditorily and in writing. With certain tasks assigned to the group, consensus may be arrived at through use of a brainstorming list.

Total-Class Brainstorming Bash. If the paper is folded with more than one task to complete on the sheet, give the instruction for the first section. Assign a time for completion and a signal for the group to give when they are finished. Then go to the next set of instructions. This continues throughout the completion of the poster.

Adjustable-Assignment Brainstorming Bash. Give specific agenda sheets so that each small group can complete its brainstorming posters with the group's specific tasks.

Community Clusters

Community clusters use small groups to discuss strategies or to share personal thoughts, products, or facts. If the assignment calls for conversations, the teacher can decide the length of the conversation and can ask the students to stand in a "talking circle." Groups work best when they have no more than four students. If the students are sharing products or an artifact, they should form a circle at a table, on the floor, or at a desk cluster.

This group may be used to

- Share work findings
- Prepare a side of an issue for debate
- Process, reflect, and give input into the lesson
- Share personal information

Content Talk

Form small groups. Divide the assignment up and let each group be in charge of reading, discussing, or preparing the assigned section with the total group. Assign roles so the responsibility is shared and the groups get the assignment done.

Research Probes

This assignment is given with a chosen or assigned topic to research. Students often need to come to consensus in their groups, choosing what they want to research. Then the desire to find out more about the topic is there. Encourage groups to divide up the assignment among group members.

For example, one student might go to the media center or resource table and look up the information. Another does a Web search, and another interviews and gathers information. Still another student might be the one they give all the found facts to and who records and organizes the data.

Experiment, Lab, Center, Station, or Project Groups

Usually groups of two or three students form the most productive working teams. Sometimes this kind of group is used because of limited resources and materials, for example, technology equipment, media materials, lab supplies, or manipulatives. Students share information, work together, and produce a product, solve a problem, or learn new methods or processes.

Multiage Grouping

Groups are formed of different ages to learn from each other and work together. For instance, student groups of different age levels can work together with a common goal and learn. This establishes a potential mentoring situation or at least brings unique perspectives from the different age levels that interact with each other. This strategy is useful for reading, computer buddies, and problem-solving groups. Several teachers at different grade levels can facilitate the grouping of multiage students. Multiage grouping can also be used to enhance project work and investigation. The diversity of ages brings unique background experiences and knowledge to the tasks. Students learn from role models. Acquisition of language and creative ideas are often shared in these mixed groups.

Remember! Tap into learning potential! Throughout their lives, students will need to work alone and with others. Learners need experiences in all group types to become effective working citizens in tomorrow's world. Teachers choose the type of group that is appropriate given the task, needs of the students, and targeted standards.

Adjusting, compacting, and grouping are important aspects of the differentiated classroom that meets a diverse audience with a curriculum that is more "sized to fit."

Consider a unit of work that you will be teaching in the near future.

1. What are the expectations or standards to be taught?

2. What assessment tools could you use to get data about students' prior knowledge, skills, and interests related to these standards?

3. Complete an adjustable grid to represent the information acquired that is related to the content or skill.

4. What instructional decisions will you make responding to the data that you have organized?

JUST AS EACH LEARNER IS UNIQUE AND ONE SIZE DOESN'T FIT ALL, teachers realize that they need a wide repertoire of instructional strategies from which to pick and choose, adjust and modify. Taking a nip and tuck here and there in a garment is a beginning, but alterations are necessary if the garment is to fit comfortably and be wearable.

Although uniqueness is an issue, there are some things we know about how the brain works: It attends to new stimuli, processes information, and stores it in memory.

HOW THE BRAIN WORKS

Let us first examine the process so that we consider it as we think about differentiated instruction. One piece of vital information from brain research is that the brain continues to grow and thrive throughout life from external stimulation in the environment (Kotulak, 1996). The brain is "plastic," which means it changes continually and grows dendrites (tree-branch–like connections) between the neurons in response to environmental stimuli and experiences.

Brains change physically in classrooms where students are engaged in meaningful, stimulating experiences. Information is taken into the brain by the senses; this usually is referred to as *sensory memory*. This is important for survival in the environment. It lasts for approximately three-fourths of a second.

Attention

Of the five senses, visual, tactile, and auditory are the most efficient in capturing attention. There are many environmental factors constantly bombarding our sensory fields to capture our attention. Novelty, color, humor, and hands-on activity all grab the attention of the learner. Emotion also plays a large role in increasing attention. Positive or negative emotions may be the hook that generates attention or engagement. Strong negative "baggage," such as a bully in the schoolyard or a problem from home, may actually block the attention needed to focus on learning. On the other hand, fun, laughter, play, and a high-challenge/low-threat environment help focus attention and maintain it.

Memory

Sensory input is either dumped out or is passed on to short-term or working memory if the individual's attention is captured.

Once attention takes data from the sensory memory to the short-term or working memory, the data are said to be *conscious*. The data last in conscious short-term memory up to 20 seconds unless we process them in some way.

We know that at the mental age of 15 years, the short-term working memory has the capacity for seven bits of information plus or minus two (Miller, 1956; Pascal-Leon, 1980). Capacity develops over the years, starting at age 5 with two spaces and increasing one space every other year until age 15. One way to deal with more than seven bits is to chunk them into larger pieces that hold more bits.

Rehearsal

Processing in working memory is often called *rehearsal*. Rehearsal or practice allows us to organize, analyze, make sense of, and remember the information. Rehearsal may be in one of two forms, *rote* (repeating information in the same form) or *elaborative* (connecting information with known data or embedding it in context).

Elaborative rehearsal facilitates organizing and associating information into networks that are then stored in long-term (unconscious) memory. Rote memory may work for some learning, like multiplication facts that are drilled and memorized and put into automatic memory, but for enduring understanding (Wiggins & McTighe, 1998) to occur, students need more than drill and kill.

Rote learning does not always have a very long shelf life because it has few hooks in the long-term memory. However, the brain is a pattern-seeking device and enjoys making meaning and connections between new ideas and those previously learned. Thus elaborative rehearsal strategies have a greater chance of producing long-term memories.

Rote rehearsal includes

- Practice
- Recitation
- Drill

Elaborative rehearsal includes

- Mnemonics
- Graphic organizers
- Role-plays/Simulations
- Rhymes/Raps
- Centers and projects
- Using multiple intelligences
- Problems/Inquiry
- Performances
- Exhibitions

Context

Context is an important contributor to memory and learning. A field trip to a farm or science center creates strong emotional hooks as well as enriched sensory stimulation. All these aspects will help solidify these experiences and concepts in the mind. *Episodic memory* is a term used to describe contextual or locale learning (O'Keefe & Nadel, 1978). It is processed through the hippocampus, as is *declarative memory,* which is concerned with the facts (who, what, where, when, and how).

Students often recall information better in the room in which they learned it. The context of the learning brings back vivid experiences of the learning that took place there. Students seem to do better on tests that are taken in the room in which they learned or studied. They also may do better on tests if the teacher who taught them is present in the room.

Emotions

Emotions play a large part not only in garnering attention but also in memory and learning. The amygdala, the brain's emotional sentinel (Goleman, 1995), imprints memory when experiences evoke strong emotions (LeDoux, 1996). Many key events in life and in schools are punctuated by and charged with emotions. For example, we all remember where we were when we heard about the 2001 attack on New York's Twin Towers. This combination of context and emotion creates vivid memories.

Associating Concepts

A way to help students deal with massive amounts of content is to organize information around concepts. For example, students can organize networks of association under concept headings such as Change, Relationships, Persuasion, and Community. These mental concept files can be accessed, and a flood of information will be released as they are opened.

Concepts also help students see the bigger picture, organize the information, and deepen their understanding. Information is organized in networks of association throughout the neocortex and is unconscious until retrieved back to working memory.

When a "file of birthdays" is opened, for example, all the facts, thoughts, images, memories, and emotions dealing with birthdays come into conscious awareness. The neural network is searched and asked to recall all it remembers. One idea triggers another. This is why the process of brainstorming is a useful tool for activating prior knowledge. The brain scans the files, and one idea brings about another as the connections are revisited.

Recall and Rehearsal

Three things can occur after data have spent time in short-term memory. They may be dumped out (because they have no meaning for the learner or the learner wasn't given any practice), they may be practiced further, or they may be transferred to long-term memory. Once in long-term memory, the data can last forever, but if not used, they will become hard to retrieve over time (Pinker, 1998). "Use it or lose it" is true in this case.

Students often need many opportunities to recall and rehearse, many times and in many ways, to deepen their understanding. Doyle and Strauss (1976, p. 25) suggest that we give people too much gum to chew (content) and not enough time to chew it (process). Maybe what we need to retain valuable information is "less gum, more chewing," as suggested in workshops by Bob Garnstom, well-known educator and organizational change consultant.

To retrieve information from long-term memory usually takes between 3 and 5 seconds, depending on its quantity and complexity. This is why "wait time" (Rowe, 1988) is so important when asking questions. Because information is stored all over the neocortex in networks of association, it takes time to search those neural networks and bring long-term unconscious memory back to short-term conscious memory (see Figure 29).

Figure 29.   Learning and Remembering New Information: A Complex Process

New information (for example, a new flower species) that captures sensory attention (sight, smell, touch, etc.) can be transferred to short-term conscious memory (1). There it can trigger the retrieval of other data (2) already stored in long-term conscious memory about other flower species, in effect opening "flower" files with previous information that have been stored throughout the neocortex (3). By examining and relating the new data to previously learned data, the newer information can be transferred to long-term memory (4), that is, it can be learned and remembered.

Long-term memory is really of two types: declarative and procedural.

Declarative	*Procedural*
The "Facts"	"Autopilot"
Who?	Things one does without thinking
What?	• playing the piano
Where?	• riding a bicycle
Why?	• doing up buttons
When?	• using the computer

Declarative memory is more conscious, whereas *procedural memory* is unconscious. Procedural memory starts as declarative. For example, when one learns to use a computer, each step is conscious and deliberate. Each step is in declarative memory: turn on switch, wait for screen, insert disk, double-click on icon. After many repetitions, the process becomes automatic and can be done unconsciously. These procedures are stored in the cerebellum (little brain). Students require lots of practice to send information and procedures to long-term memory. Practice may occur in a multitude of ways using a variety of multiple intelligences and as many modalities as possible to involve opportunities for visual, auditory, and tactile/kinesthetic learners to develop understanding.

PLANNING INSTRUCTIONAL STRATEGIES

Information about the process of memory is useful for teachers as they plan programs for a diverse group of students so that the students can realize their potential. Teachers may want to ask themselves the following questions as they plan:

- What do I want students to know or be able to do as a result of this learning experience?
- How will we judge success?
- What do they already know and what are they able to do?
- How can attention be captured and sustained?
- What will the "emotional hook" be for the learners?
- How will new information and skills be acquired?
- How will students practice or rehearse to make meaning and understanding?
- How will they receive ongoing feedback during and after the learning?

FOCUS ACTIVITIES

If teachers are going to capture students' attention, they need strategies to do so. Focus activities will

- Help the learner focus and pay attention
- Eliminate distracters
- Open "mental files"
- Provide choices
- Encourage self-directed learning
- Capitalize on "prime time"
- Fill unallocated time—extend or enrich or "sponge" up extra time

Using focus activities at the beginning of class helps students block out distracters, concentrate on activating prior knowledge, and sustain attention. Focus activities can take many forms. One teacher in a math class asked students to do the following with a paper and pencil:

- ✓ Pick a number from 1 to 9.
- ✓ Multiply it by 9.
- ✓ Add the two digits.
- ✓ Take away 5.
- ✓ Locate the corresponding letter in the alphabet.
- ✓ Pick a country that begins with that letter.
- ✓ Pick an animal that begins with the last letter of the country.
- ✓ Pick a color that begins with the last letter of your animal.

Then the teacher asked the students if they had an orange kangaroo in Denmark.

"Wow," they exclaimed, "How did you know that?" "You figure it out," she challenged them. They eagerly worked in pairs and analyzed the process and discovered that when you multiply any number by 9, the resulting two digits add up to 9. Then when you subtract 5 you get 4. The number 4 leads you to D. Under pressure, most people choose Denmark as a country. The last letter is K and kangaroo usually comes to mind. The last letter of kangaroo being O leads to the color orange. Then the teacher continued on with reviewing the multiplication table for 9. This teacher knew how to make learning fun, add novelty to the learning, and challenge the students to solve a problem. The brain loves to make sense and seek patterns in information or processes.

In another classroom, the teacher had students begin the class by writing down on a small card or paper:

- Three things I learned yesterday . . .
- Two ideas that connected for me . . .
- One question I still have . . .

K-W-L

Often, teachers use a K-W-L chart (Ogle, 1986). The K stands for what students already know about the topic. The W stands for what the students want to know. The L is used at the end of the lesson or unit of study to enable students to reflect on their learning and identify the information and processes learned.

This strategy opens up mental files to see what students already know, as well as creating anticipation and curiosity about the new learning to come. It also brings closure and satisfaction at the end of the unit of study as they reflect and articulate their learnings.

Other Strategies for Focusing

Other focus activities can take many forms. They may include challenges, questions and problems, or journal entries. Tasks may be offered that require recall and application of previously learned information. For example, students who had read a chapter for homework were asked to sit with a buddy and find as many "feeling" words as they could in the chapter that helped develop the reader's understanding of the character.

Sometimes, teachers offer choices to students in order to capitalize on their interests and give them options. These techniques are also forms of pre-assessment that help the teacher and students set goals and design and select learning tasks appropriate to individuals or groups of learners.

The following example is a set of focus tasks that a teacher offered to students to allow them to make a choice.

From the chapter that you read last night, choose one of the following tasks and work alone or with a partner to complete it:

✓ Draw a comic strip to show the events in the chapter.

✓ In your journal, chronicle the events in the chapter.

✓ Describe the setting and how it related to the events in the chapter.

✓ If you were a newscaster, what would your progress report be?

✓ Rewrite a passage of the chapter in your own words. Use synonyms to replace some of the author's words.

SPONGE ACTIVITIES

Throughout the day, there may be times when students finish work early. The teacher can offer other tasks to "sponge" up the extra time without wasting instructional time. Tasks may also be provided for students to use as sponge activities when extra time is available. These tasks are also useful when the teacher is working with one group and students in other groups finish what they were doing. These sponge activities help students become more self-directed learners. Sometimes, the students will focus on a personal quest or project that they are pursuing or some standard or skill that they are trying to master. Broader or more general tasks may be offered, such as the following:

- Develop a crossword puzzle on the computer to review the topic.
- Use the computer to develop a word web on this concept or topic.
- Revise your agenda for the week.
- Work on your culminating task for the unit.
- Use a word web to organize the ideas in this unit.
- Examine the items in your portfolio and make some decisions regarding the pieces you have included. Should some be deleted or replaced at this point?

These more generic tasks may be posted for the week for all to refer to when they have some time to "sponge" up productively.

Focus or sponge activities should all be related to the objectives in the learning process, not just fun activities. They may be fun, but they should be focused on the necessary content or skills students should be developing.

GRAPHIC ORGANIZERS

Graphic organizers and cooperative group learning are among the instructional strategies that the McREL research shows can lead to huge gains in student achievement (Marzano, Pickering, & Pollack, 2001). The chart in Figure 30 lists the instructional strategies that McREL recommends along with what we know about the brain that tends to support the strategies' success. The center column looks at what we know. In the right-hand column, we have added tactics used in the classroom as part of larger strategies to support student learning in the differentiated classroom.

What Are They?

Graphic organizers are useful thinking tools that allow students to organize information and allow students to see their thinking. They are visual/spatial, logical/mathematical tools that appeal to many learners for managing and organizing information. Graphic organizers give visual representations of facts/concepts and also show the relationships between and among new facts and previous information. They are also used to plot processes and procedures. Graphic organizers can be used at many points in the lesson.

Why Use Them?

The difference between good and poor learners is not the sheer quantity of what the good learner learns, but rather the good learner's ability to organize and use information (Smith, 1986).

Figure 30.   Instructional Strategies for Improving Student Achievement: Best Practice, Brain Research, and Teaching Tactics (see also Marzano et al., 2001)

Strategy	Percentile Gain	How the Brain Works	Strategies
Comparing, contrasting, classifying, analogies, and metaphors	45	The brain seeks patterns, connections, and relationships between and among prior and new learning.	• Classifying • Compare, contrast • Venn diagrams • Synectics • Concept attainment • Concept formation
Summarizing and note taking	34	The brain pays attention to meaningful information and deletes that which is not relevant.	• Mind maps • Word webs • Jigsaw • Reciprocal
Reinforcing effort and providing recognition	29	The brain responds to challenge and not threat. Emotions enhance learning.	• Stories of determination • Celebrate successes
Assigning homework and practice	28	If you don't use it, you lose it. Practice and rehearsal make learning "stick."	• Create challenges in a variety of ways
Generating nonlinguistic representations	27	The brain is a parallel processor. Visual stimuli are recalled with 90% accuracy.	• Mind maps • Graphic organizers • Models
Using cooperative learning	27	The brain is social. Collaboration facilitates understanding and higher-order thinking.	• Think-Pair-Share • Jigsaw • P.I.G.S.F.
Setting objectives and providing feedback	23	The brain responds to high challenge and continues to strive based on feedback.	• Helpful feedback • Rubrics • Criteria • Expectations
Generating and testing hypotheses	23	The brain is curious and has an innate need to make meaning through patterns.	• Problem-based inquiry • Portfolios • Case studies
Providing questions, cues, and advance organizers	22	The brain responds to wholes and parts. All learners need to open "mental files" into which new learning can be "hooked."	• Wait time • Questioning techniques • Agenda maps • Advance organizers • Diagrams and charts

Source: Copyright © 2006 by Corwin Press. Reprinted with permission from *Designing Brain Compatible Learning* (3rd ed.), by Gayle H. Gregory & Terence Parry.

Graphic organizers can be used

- For brainstorming at the beginning of a lesson or unit to find out what students already know
- With reading assignments or when watching a video so that students can organize and capture information. The teacher may provide one, or students can design their own using the criteria given by the teacher, such as Who? What? Where? and Why?
- To help chronicle a sequence of events or a process
- To relate new information to previously learned information
- To check for understanding
- For note taking and summarizing
- For the culminating assessment

How Do We Use Them?

As with any tool, students need to be taught how to use the organizer and be given opportunities for practice with a full range of content and situations. Teachers model how the organizer can be used with content that is not too complicated. That way, students learn the process of using the organizer and can then use it with any content. Over time, students become familiar with the process of using a variety of graphic organizers. They will become adept at choosing appropriate organizers to fit the situation. Many students begin to design and create their own organizers to fit their needs. Using visual representations often appeals to the intrapersonal learner, who appreciates opportunities for processing and reflecting on new information independently. Organizers can be used independently, with a partner, or in a small group.

Effective Graphic Organizers for Comparing and Contrasting

Comparing, contrasting, classifying, and using metaphors are instructional strategies that increase student achievement (Marzano et al., 2001). Students who spend time looking at the similarities and differences between two topics and perhaps plot these on a graphic organizer deepen their understanding and ability to use the knowledge.

Venn Diagram

The often-used Venn diagram (see Figure 31) identifies what is similar and what is different between two topics. A quick way to teach students to use the Venn is to have them compare themselves with a classmate as to personal characteristics, likes and dislikes, hobbies or sports, pets, and so on. They can brainstorm these characteristics individually and then plot them on the Venn with their partners, placing similarities in the overlapping center and the differences on each side.

Comparison Matrix

A *comparison matrix* (see Figure 32) is another way to compare several items based on identified criteria. For example, when comparing states, the following could be listed

Figure 31.   Venn Diagram: Used to Identify an Area of Overlap Between Two Topics

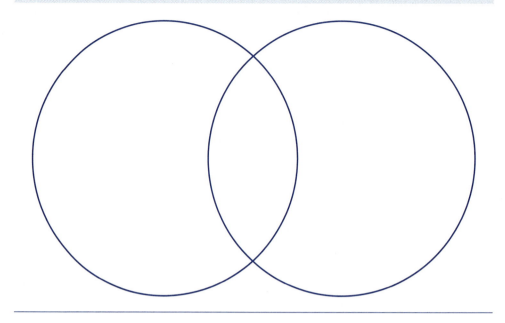

Figure 32.   Cross-Classification Compare and Contrast Matrix

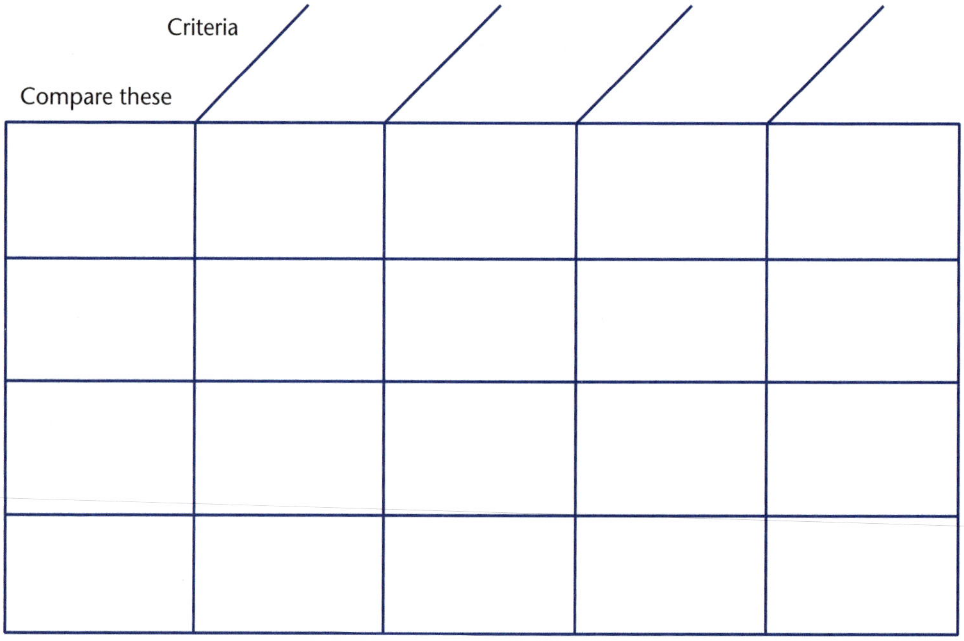

Criteria

Compare these

in the left column: New York, Arizona, California, and Louisiana. Across the top, the following criteria could be considered: climate, population, geography, and size. This information, once plotted, can be transferred to a Venn diagram to identify the similarities and differences between two of the states.

Comparing Two Things

Other forms of comparing and contrasting can be used. In Figure 33, any two things, ideas, concepts, or procedures may be scrutinized. At the top, in the first two frames, the two things being analyzed are put in place. In the two large boxes underneath, all their attributes are listed. Then all their similarities are selected and placed in the large frame underneath the "Similarities" heading. Finally, the ways in which the concepts differ are placed in the appropriate frames. Use the numbers so that the items in each box that differ correspond to one another. Students can compare forms of art, continents, scientific procedures, politicians, or historical events or any two pieces of content in any subject area.

Word Webs

The *word web* is an organizer that can be used for organizing and classifying. It enables students to focus on a concept, theme, or topic; identify the secondary categories related to the big idea; and then add all the significant dimensions related to those secondary categories. In Figure 34, for example, the big idea is World War II; and the secondary categories are the Axis, the Allies, Causes, Differences, Theaters of War, the Blitzkrieg, and Pivotal Events.

The quality of thinking, classifying, and deep understanding that it takes to create an intricate word web is a form of elaborative thinking and processing, as shown in Figure 35.

Figure 33.   Comparing 2 Things Flow Chart

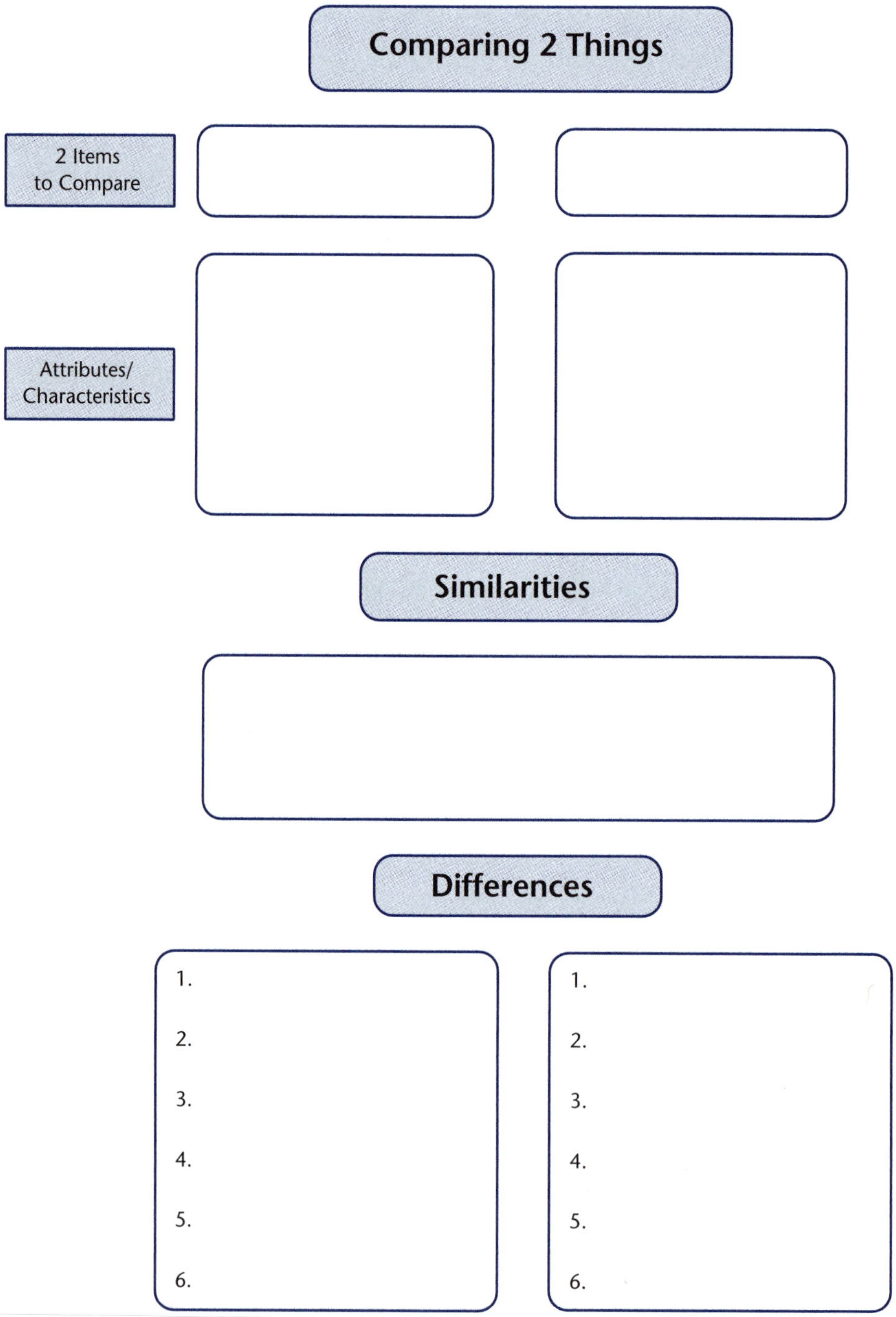

Comparing 2 Things

2 Items to Compare		

Attributes/ Characteristics		

Similarities

Differences

1.	1.
2.	2.
3.	3.
4.	4.
5.	5.
6.	6.

Figure 34. Example of a Word Web Used to Organize and Classify Primary and Secondary Concepts Related to World War II

A word web can be used to assess how well students have organized data. It also indicates that they have grasped the major concepts and made connections between them. It is also a useful tool to organize thinking in the prewriting stage.

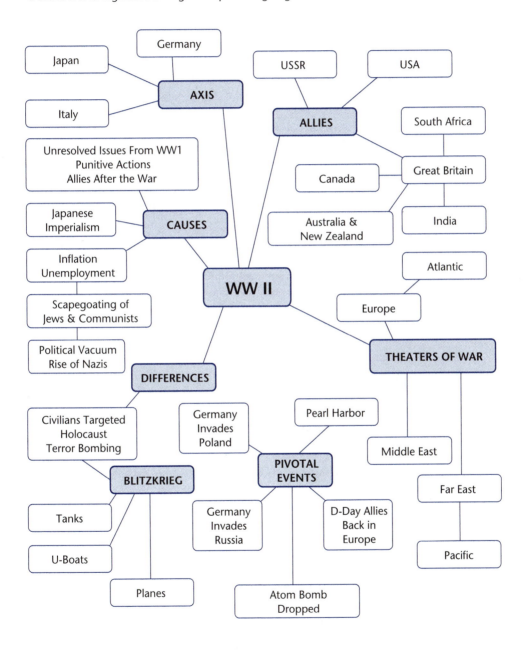

SOURCE: Used with permission from Terence Parry.

Figure 35.   Graphic Organizer Framework

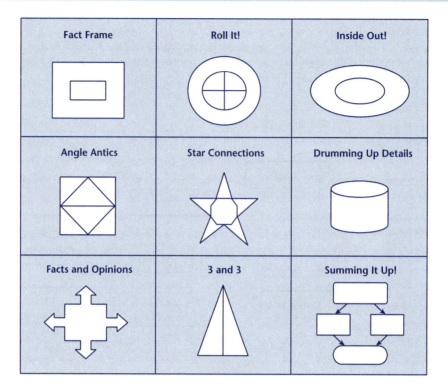

1. Fact Frame: Write fact in center box. Write supporting details in outer box.

2. Roll It! Write topic in the tire section. Write four key points in the spokes.

3. Inside Out! Write an important event, object, character, or place in the center. Write its attributes in the outer oval.

4. Angle Antics: Put a cause in each big triangle. Write the effects on each side of the cause.

5. Star Connections: Place the topic in the middle. Add a key fact in each star point.

6. Drumming Up Details: Write a prediction on the top of the drum. State the outcomes or learned facts on the side of the drum.

7. Fact and Opinions: Write the fact in the center. List an opinion by each arrow.

8. 3 and 3: Write an important topic vocabulary noun in each of the large triangles. Write the meaning, a sentence, and draw a picture on the sidelines.

9. Summing It Up! In the top rectangle, write the fact. In the next two boxes, write two supporting details. Then write the summary or conclusion in the bottom figure.

METAPHORICAL AND ANALOGOUS THINKING

Using metaphors and analogies is another way to show similarities and differences and to connect new information to more familiar objects or concepts. In Chapter 3, "Knowing the Learner," we used the objects beach ball, microscope, clipboard, and puppy to help clarify and understand the characteristics of the four styles of learning. By thinking of these four objects, students can easily recall the attributes of each of the objects and in turn relate those characteristics to the four learning styles to understand them better.

Students can also relate new information by connecting it to something with which they are familiar. They may be able to understand the Renaissance if we ask them to explain how the Renaissance is like a video game, or understand the government if we ask them how the government is like an orchestra. When using two seemingly unrelated ideas or topics, we are causing students to examine comparisons and look at the similarities and differences between the two.

Having students stretch their thinking through metaphorical connections increases the likelihood of broadening their understanding of a concept or topic and remembering it in the future.

COOPERATIVE GROUP LEARNING

Cooperative group learning is one of the most researched instructional strategies in education today. We have gained valuable insight over the years from revered educators such as Aronson (1978); Bellanca and Fogarty (1991); Bennett, Rolheiser-Bennett, and Stevahn (1991); Cantelon (1991a, 1991b); Clarke, Wideman, and Eadie (1990); Johnson, Johnson, and Holubec (1998); and Kagan (1992). Working in cooperative groups, students learn valuable social skills, use higher-order thinking, and rehearse and practice new concepts, processes, and information. Cooperative group learning does not happen successfully unless it is well orchestrated and certain considerations prevail. These considerations increase the chances that the groups will work well together and achieve targeted standards (Johnson et al., 1998).

The acronym TASK (Robbins, Gregory, & Herndon, 2000) can be used to remember these aspects of cooperative group learning:

T Thinking is built into the process.

A Accountability is essential. Goal achievement: both individual and group.

S Social skills lead to team success.

K Keep everyone on TASK: roles, tasks, resources, novelty, simulations, and clear expectations.

Thinking Skills Are Built Into the Process

Cooperative group learning is ideal for embedding a variety of other instructional strategies that make a difference in student learning. Graphic organizers, thinking skills, and metaphors are easily used in cooperative group work to facilitate rehearsal and practice. Groups can be given tasks that are differentiated and adjusted to levels of the thinking taxonomy, a topic that we will discuss in detail later in this chapter. This will challenge groups at a variety of levels. Cubing, another topic we will discuss later in this chapter, also works well in cooperative group situations. Opportunities to explore content by using some or all of the multiple intelligences are possible. Students see many sides of a topic when using multiple intelligences as a lens.

Accountability Is Essential

Students who work together in cooperative groups generally produce a group product or a project that is graded. Each student needs to be accountable for his or her personal contributions to the group and also for personal acquisition of knowledge and skills as a result of the group process. Teachers often use checklists or journal entries to collect data on the contributions and learning of individuals in the group. If teachers need to know what students know and have learned in the group session, individual tests, quizzes, demonstrations, exhibitions, and conferences will help clarify the understanding and competencies of each of the students. Cooperative group learning is a powerful strategy for learning, but we can't assume that everyone will know and understand the content and develop the skills just by being in a group.

Assessment may be multifaceted and include

- An individual grade for the piece of work completed or the part of the presentation given
- A group grade for the final product or presentation
- A test or quiz on the content
- A mark for group participation

Consider the cooperative learning activity a learning experience. It is another way to blend the individual needs with the learning, discussion, process, and investigation of the information. Then give an individual assessment to see what each learner knows about the information. This way, the work and the individual's grade are not dependent on the other group members. Group grades often cause problems and may create "social loafers."

Social Skills for Team Success

Even though teachers work to build climate and trust in the classroom, they may also need to teach social skills. Cooperative group learning not only helps students learn content and competencies but also helps them develop their emotional intelligence in the five domains (Goleman, 1995):

- Self-awareness: through reflection
- Self-motivation: developing persistence and a positive work ethic
- Managing emotions: learning strategies for conflict resolution and consensus building
- Empathy: listening, reflecting feelings, and behaving in a supportive manner
- Social skills: opportunities to identify practice and reflect on social skills

Students have different needs in these areas, and teachers will observe where those needs are as they monitor groups and recognize the strengths and weaknesses of their students.

Basic social skills that students need include

- Using appropriate language
- Speaking politely and quietly
- Encouraging others
- Listening to others
- Asking for help

Some social skills that students need to function well in a group include

- Disagreeing in an agreeable way
- Accepting different opinions
- Following procedures
- Checking for accuracy and understanding
- Dealing with conflict

Students need to know what a social skill "looks like, sounds like and feels like" (Hill & Hancock, 1993) through conscious identification of the skill, modeling, practice, and feedback.

Teachers often post charts for reference that describe acceptable behavior in the class-room. Students need to contribute to the charts using their own language and terms. This increases clarity and ownership of the behavior and the probability that it will be practiced. Figure 36 is an example of a chart that describes listening to others. It was developed by a teacher and students during a conversation about the importance of listening to other people in a group.

Figure 36.   Social Skill: Listening to Others

Looks like	Sounds like	Feels like
Looking at the person Nodding and smiling	Tell me more . . . Mmm . . .	I've been heard My ideas are valued

Students then need to practice this skill with their groups and reflect on its use.

Individuals learn differently as a result of their experience and need a chance to contemplate their learning and their participation. Because students sometimes don't have the ability for reflection without guidelines, an organizer may be provided. Figure 37 is an example of student reflection after a group effort.

Figure 37.   Reflection on Group Work

Date: _____

Name: _____

In my math class today we were involved in a cooperative learning activity.
This is a summary of what my group did.

My role was . . .

_____

_____

My behavior in that role was . . .

_____

_____

I helped achieve the group goal by . . .

_____

_____

I could have . . .

_____

_____

One thing I need to work on is . . .

_____

_____

Keeping Students on Task

Students in cooperative groups usually are assigned roles that increase the chances that they will work interdependently (Johnson et al., 1998). Roles can be assigned to keep the group functioning well, such as encourager, clarifier, summarizer, or questioner. Other roles may include those that facilitate the task, such as recorder, reader, researcher, drawer, materials manager, or reporter. This encourages students to take responsibility and ownership for the task by assuming a particular role.

Some teachers may want to set up a scenario more like the real world and assign some of the following roles to the students in a cooperative group (from Kathy & Rob Bocchino, Heart of Change Consultants, workshop strategy).

Production Manager. The production manager is responsible for the project. You will oversee and ensure that the other managers are working appropriately. You will manage the process, keep track of progress, and be the only person in the group who communicates with the CEO (teacher) when the group needs clarification or direction.

Information Manager. Your job is to ensure the accuracy and quality of the product. Your listening skills are valuable assets and help you make sure you clarify what the client is asking for. You will make sure all group members understand the client's/CEO's expectations. You must adhere to any written directions.

Resource Manager. Your job is to gather and manage the materials necessary to complete the group project. Make sure all group papers and materials are properly stored away at the end of the period. If other objects, props, or materials are necessary, arrange to acquire them and make sure they are available when needed.

Personnel Manager. Your job is to manage the people on the team and build morale throughout the production. Encourage other team members, manage conflicts, and facilitate problem solving when necessary. Monitor for effort and productivity. Communicate any concerns to the production manager.

Technology Manager. Your job is to assist group members with all technical aspects of the production. You will assist members with their computer skills when using the Internet for research, with spreadsheets and databases, word processing, presentation techniques, and troubleshooting.

Time Manager. Your job is to know when all deadlines are and remind others in the production team of those deadlines. You will keep a log of the steps and the progress. Communicate with the production manager concerning timelines and concerns. Communicate with the production manager concerning a particular team member who is not meeting time requirements. If more time is needed, ask the production manager to negotiate for more time.

The "Keeping Students on Task Bookmarks" in Figure 38 can be given to team members to help them keep focused on their duties for team success.

Figure 38.   Keeping Students on Task Bookmarks

Production Manager will:
- oversee the project
- ensure everyone does his or her job
- manage the process
- keep track of the project
- communicate with the teacher when group needs direction

Information Manager will:
- ensure accuracy of materials
- ensure quality of the product
- listen and make sure ideas are clear
- follow written directions

Resource Manager will:
- gather and manage materials
- properly store materials
- arrange and acquire materials and make sure materials are available

Creating Interdependence and Building Alliances Within Groups

Teachers also can increase the interdependence in the groups

- By creating a sequence to the process: Each group member has a role and particular step to perform in the task.

- By providing limited resources (tools, texts, materials) that must be shared to complete the activity.

- By providing novelty and engaging scenarios or simulations in which students take on personas, such as investigator, researcher, or land developer. This creates a role that would be found in the real world and often adds authenticity to the activity.

There are many times when students work in cooperative groups of two, three, or four. In fact, working in pairs is a great way for students to build alliances in the classroom, by getting to work with many students to get to know them. It is also hard to get left out of a pair (Johnson et al., 1998). Partner work gives students a chance to practice social skills in a controlled environment with only one other personality at a time. It also builds community as students get to know one another one-on-one.

Whenever cooperative group learning is used as a vehicle for student learning, teachers need to ask the following questions to clarify the intention and process for the learning:

- What is it that students need to accomplish, and how will I communicate that? (Written task cards or charted directions should be clearly outlined for students so that expectations are clear and visible to all.)

- What will the size of the group be, considering the task?

Figure 38. (Continued)

Personnel Manager will:	Technology Manager will:	Time Manager will:
• manage people and build morale • encourage team members • help resolve conflicts • help solve problems • monitor effort and productivity	• assist with technology aspects • help with computer needs • resources from Internet • help with presentation techniques	• manage deadlines • help team keep on track • communicate with production manager • negotiate time needed

- How will I group students and why? (randomly, by ability, by background knowledge, heterogeneous but structured; see Figure 27, "Stick Picks," and Figure 28, "Wagon Wheel Teaming," in Chapter 5)

- What social skill will they practice and reflect on? (The social skill should be relevant to the task.)

- How will they learn about the social skill?

- How will they monitor its use?

- What are the timelines and guidelines for the task?

- What assessment will be used for the academic task? (presentation, product, report, performance, exhibition, test, quiz, etc.)

- What roles or tasks will group members be assigned to ensure interdependence and active participation?

- Are the groups functional?

- Do the groups get along socially?

Jigsaw

Another way to increase interdependence is by using a *jigsaw method*. Jigsaw (Aronson, 1978; Slavin, 1994; see Figure 39) is a very effective strategy, but not one that would be used with students until they have the social skills to deal with several members in a group as well as the skills to work independently. It is a powerful strategy for covering more material in less time. It enhances learning and increases retention. Students begin in a base group of three or four and are given letters or numbers or names that will help them form expert groups. In the expert group, students are to access information or learn new material or

Figure 39.   Jigsaw Strategy: Used to Enhance Interdependence
With More Advanced Learners

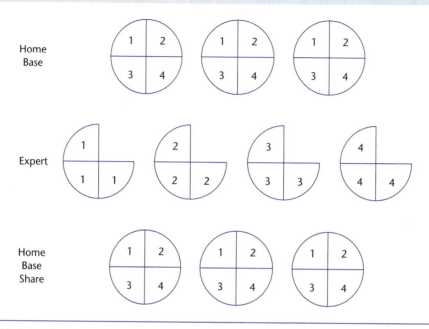

skills that they will in turn teach to their base group. When they return to the base group, they teach their group members what they have learned.

Individual accountability is built into the process by having each member hand in a report, test, or quiz on the material learned or by calling on students randomly to report for their group.

The jigsaw method facilitates the sharing of responsibility for learning. It helps focus energy in a task and provides structure and process for the learning. It has inter- and intra-personal components that also allow students to process information and move and interact with a variety of class members to gain a greater perspective on the knowledge or skills that are targeted for learning. It offers many chances for elaborative rehearsal and use of higher-order thinking through dialogue.

Jigsaws can be differentiated for students by giving them different materials and content to match different levels of readiness. Products, projects, or other authentic tasks and assessment that are expected from the group, based on their preferences and multiple intelligences, offer another way to differentiate.

The following example is a way of building in all the aspects of TASK.

The "Character Sketch" (see Figure 40) is an organizer that can be used by a cooperative group of four people when reading a story or novel. Groups A and B would focus on the same character (perhaps the main character). Groups C and D would identify a different character, and so on. The base group (Persons 1, 2, 3, and 4) would cut the organizer on the broken line and distribute the four sections. Each person in Group A would meet with the same number partner from Group B (i.e., 1 with 1, 2 with 2, 3 with 3, and 4 with 4). They would discuss an aspect of the character depending on the section of the organizer that they have. For example, two students may have the quadrant that says, "Looks like." They would find evidence in the story of what the character looks like and then write their conclusions in that segment of the quadrant. As they work together, the social skill they would use would be to clarify information and listen to others' ideas. Each group of partners would meet and complete their sections of the organizer: "Looks like," "Seems like," "Does," and "Sounds like." Then the base groups would reconstitute and review all the evidence and conclusions that they made. From this information, the group would write a complete character sketch based on all the attributes collected.

The organizer can be reproduced on large chart paper to increase the space for collected information and to allow all participants to see the information. Each group member would have an organizer to collect data personally from other expert team members. This activity is an example of a jigsaw. There is interdependence built in through shared resources and tasks. The students practice social skills as they work. They access information and use evidence to support their thinking, both worthy standards in any classroom.

This organizer can also be modified and used to divide tasks in other subject areas in a jigsaw process as well. Students could begin in a base group and examine four aspects of a country, such as food, peoples, geography, and origins (or in biology, they could focus on body systems, such as respiratory, digestive, nervous, and circulatory) in their expert groups and bring that information back to their base groups.

Questions Often Asked About Cooperative Group Learning

What Is the Best Way to Group Students?

If a group of students get along socially, they usually get the job done. Occasionally let students choose partners or small groups. Group work is not always a social decision. Students also need to develop skills to work with a variety of personalities and perspectives. Alternate with random grouping and self-selected and teacher-constructed groups.

What Do You Do With the Student Who Does Not Want to Work in a Group?

An independent learner, who usually does not like group work, works better with a partner than a larger group. Remember this student is learning important social skills when working with others. He or she does need some independent work time to process the cognitive learning.

What Is the Best-Sized Group?

Students working in groups of twos, threes, or fours are the most successful. When needing consensus, use groups of three to break the tie. Remember that the size of the group is also decided by the task to be completed. If the task is complex, more students may be needed. However, when students are developing skills for group work, smaller groups are better. It is hard to get left out of a pair. There is less social conflict and plenty to do. There is more "airtime" for each partner, and generally students stay on task.

Figure 40.   Character Sketch: Used as an Organizer
by Four Students When Reading a Story or Novel

Character:

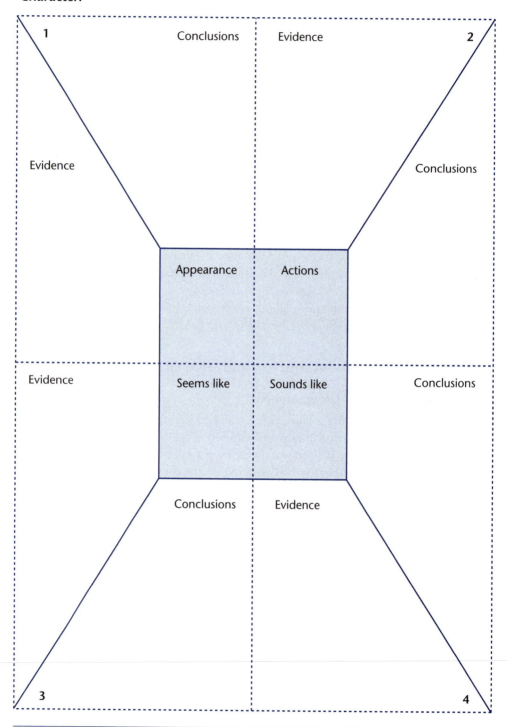

INDEPENDENT WORK ASSIGNMENTS

In every classroom, independent work is given daily. In a differentiated classroom, independent work time can be a time to meet individual gaps in the learning or challenge the students who know the information. Students are not always doing the same assignments. Some examples follow of activities that can be used as independent work assignments.

The following are samples of assignment activities for follow-ups after learning information by reading a passage or a teacher lecturette. Use these ideas to develop differentiated assignments, such as agendas, homework, centers, or projects, for the students to demonstrate what has been learned. These assignments also intensify the learners' knowledge about a standard, concept, or unit.

Record findings.

Hold a small group text talk.

Write a song.

Develop a cinquain.

Write a poem.

Develop a collage.

Find the background music.

Develop a caricature.

Develop an editorial cartoon.

Write a cartoon strip with speech bubbles.

Illustrate the ____.

Write adjectives or phrases to describe.

Develop a mural.

Play *Who Wants to be a Millionaire*.

Design a puppet.

Find the missing piece(s).

Write an editorial with your point of view.

Make a bar graph and interpret the data.

Create a pie chart and explain the results.

Develop a key.

Act out the vocabulary words.

Create a vocabulary game.

List the synonyms or antonyms.

Write a summary.

Develop a critique.

Write your opinion.

Discover how it works.

Develop the sequence.

Invent a new way.

Conduct an interview.

Discuss with a partner.

Develop questions.

Create a rap.

Write a limerick.

Write an advertisement.

Role-play.

Portray a reenactment.

Draw a picture.

Make a diorama.

Color code.

Write the attributes.

Create a timeline.

Design a new game.

Play *Jeopardy*.

Draw the setting.

Draw a map.

Use a manipulative.

Design a brochure.

Scavenge for information.

Prepare point of view.

Name the causes.

List the reasons.

Write the main idea.

Write the directions.

Draw a conclusion.

Write the fact(s).

Name examples.

Debate the issue.

Identify the sounds.

Write an ad.

DIFFERENTIATING LEVELS OF THINKING AND QUESTIONING

Undue stress can occur during teacher-student question-and-answer sessions. Fear of ridicule occurs when students are challenged by questions that are beyond their levels of understanding or comprehension. The notion of "wait time" (Rowe, 1988) gives students time to access information stored in long-term memory. We know this takes at least 3 to 5 seconds. The quality or quantity of the answer is often increased by the amount of time given in order to access the information and formulate an answer. Generally, the longer the "think time," the better the answer.

"Think, Pair, Share" (Lyman & McTighe, 1988) is a great technique to facilitate wait time. Asking students to think by themselves, pair with other students, and share their ideas naturally gives students time to think, access information, and formulate better answers. This also decreases the chances of overstressing the student and increases the chances of the student actually thinking about and attending to the question that has been posed. It encourages all students to share thinking, not just the person called on to answer. Studies show that greater retention and student achievement will result when students are given more wait time for thinking (Black, Harrison, Lee, Marshall, & Wiliam, 2004). As the teacher comes to know the learners better and to recognize their levels of readiness, questions can be differentiated by level of complexity. This challenges learners at or just beyond their levels of comprehension or experience.

Bloom's Thinking Taxonomy

Often, teachers ask questions or pose problems at different levels of Bloom's thinking taxonomy (Bloom et al., 1956), for example,

- Level 1, Knowledge-Recall: What is the story about?
- Level 2, Comprehension-Understanding: Why did this happen?
- Level 3, Application-Transfer: Use the information to predict . . .
- Level 4, Analysis-Examining: How many elements are present?
- Level 5, Synthesis-Combining: Change the story to a new setting.
- Level 6, Evaluation-Rating: Rank all the solutions in priority order.

Bloom's levels (see Figure 41) can also be used to layer the curriculum. In our lesson-planning template (see Figure 3 in Chapter 1), the levels of working with the content and skills include acquiring the knowledge or skills, applying and adjusting them in other situations, and assessing and evaluating their use.

Teachers may differentiate questions or layer curriculum based on students' readiness and levels of comprehension. Figures 41 and 42 offer samples of thinking level, definition, directing verbs, and question starters that may be used to align lessons and learning tasks with the different levels of the taxonomy.

We plan opportunities so that students interact with new knowledge and skills and develop an understanding and ability to retain and retrieve information in long-term memory. This is the learning process. By using verbs from Bloom's taxonomy, we can deepen understanding and learning using multiple rehearsals that "drill down" into the knowledge and skills. For example, related to a concept or skill, the "Potential Activities" column (see Figure 42) can guide us to work through the "Acquire, Apply and Adjust, and Assess" process.

Figure 41. Aligning Lesson Plans With the Six Levels of Bloom's Taxonomy

Lesson-Planning Steps	Thinking Level	Definition	Directing Verbs
Acquire	*Knowledge* Learn information	Recall the facts and remember previously learned information.	Describe, list, identify, locate, label
Apply	*Comprehension* Understand information	Understand the meaning of and the how and why of events.	Explain, give examples, paraphrase, summarize
Adjust	*Application* Use information	Transfer the skill or knowledge to another situation or setting. It tests knowledge and comprehension.	Infer, predict, deduce, adapt, modify, solve problems
Adjust	*Analysis* Examine parts	Break down information to specific parts so that the whole can be understood. Understanding structure can help with comparisons.	Discriminate, classify, categorize, subdivide, delineate
Adjust	*Synthesis* Use differently	Combine elements to create new and different ideas or models.	Induce, create, compose, generalize, combine, rearrange, design, plan
Assess	*Evaluation* Judge the information	Rank or rate the value of information using a set of criteria.	Judge, compare, criticize, contrast, justify, conclude

Figure 42.   Question Starters and Classroom Activities
Differentiated According to Bloom's Taxonomy

QUESTION STARTERS

POTENTIAL ACTIVITIES

Level I: **KNOWLEDGE** (recall)

1. What is the definition for . . . ?
2. What happened after . . . ?
3. Recall the facts.
4. What were the characteristics of . . . ?
5. Which is true or false?
6. How many . . . ?
7. Who was the . . . ?
8. Tell in your own words.

1. Describe the . . .
2. Make a time line of events.
3. Make a facts chart.
4. Write a list of . . . steps in . . . facts about . . .
5. List all the people in the story.
6. Make a chart showing . . .
7. Make an acrostic.
8. Recite a poem.

Level II: **COMPREHENSION**

1. Why are these ideas similar?
2. In your own words retell the story of . . .
3. What do you think could happen?
4. How are these ideas different?
5. Explain what happened after.
6. What are some examples?
7. Can you provide a definition of . . . ?
8. Who was the key character?

1. Cut out or draw pictures to show an event.
2. Illustrate what you think the main idea was.
3. Make a cartoon strip showing the sequence of . . .
4. Write and perform a play based on the . . .
5. Compare this _____with_____
6. Construct a model of . . .
7. Write a news report.
8. Prepare a flow chart to show the sequence . . .

Level III: **APPLICATION** (applying without understanding is not effective)

1. What is another instance of . . . ?
2. Demonstrate the way to . . .
3. Which one is most like . . . ?
4. What questions would you ask?
5. Which factors would you change?
6. Could this have happened in . . . ? Why or why not?
7. How would you organize these ideas?

1. Construct a model to demonstrate using it.
2. Make a display to illustrate one event.
3. Make a collection about . . .
4. Design a relief map to include relevant information about an event.
5. Scan a collection of photographs to illustrate a particular aspect of the study.
6. Create a mural to depict . . .

Figure 42. (Continued)

QUESTION STARTERS

POTENTIAL ACTIVITIES

Level IV: **ANALYSIS**

1. What are the component parts of . . . ?
2. What steps are important in the process of . . . ?
3. If . . . then . . .
4. What other conclusions can you reach about . . . that have not been mentioned?
5. The difference between the fact and the hypothesis is . . .
6. The solution would be to . . .
7. What is the relationship between . . . and . . . ?

---

1. Design a questionnaire about . . .
2. Conduct an investigation to produce . . .
3. Make a flow chart to show . . .
4. Construct a graph to show . . .
5. Put on a play about . . .
6. Review . . . in terms of identified criteria.
7. Prepare a report about the area of study.

Level V: **SYNTHESIS**

1. Can you design a . . . ?
2. Why not compose a song about . . . ?
3. Why don't you devise your own way to . . . ?
4. Can you create new and unusual uses for . . . ?
5. Can you develop a proposal for . . . ?
6. How would you deal with . . . ?
7. Invent a scheme that would . . .

---

1. Create a model that shows your new ideas.
2. Devise an original plan or experiment for . . .
3. Finish the incomplete . . .
4. Make a hypothesis about . . .
5. Change . . . so that it will . . .
6. Propose a method to . . .
7. Prescribe a way to . . .
8. Give the book a new title.

Level VI: **EVALUATION**

1. In your opinion . . .
2. Appraise the chances for . . .
3. Grade or rank the . . .
4. What do you think should be the outcome?
5. What solution do you favor and why?
6. Which systems are best? Worst?
7. Rate the relative value of these ideas to . . .
8. Which is the better bargain?

---

1. Prepare a list of criteria you would use to judge a . . . Indicate priority ratings you would give.
2. Conduct a debate about an issue.
3. Prepare an annotated bibliography . . .
4. Form a discussion panel on the topic of . . .
5. Prepare a case to present your opinions about . . .
6. List some common assumptions about . . . Rationalize your reactions.

CUBING

Cubing is another technique that can help students think at different levels of the taxonomy (Cowan & Cowan, 1980). Cubing is a technique for considering a subject from six points of view (Cowan & Cowan, 1980; Tomlinson, 2001). Cubing works well when we are locked into a particular way of thinking.

One side of the cube may say: Describe it

Another side: Compare it

The third side: Associate it

The fourth side: Analyze it

The fifth side: Apply it

And the sixth side says: Argue for or against it

Cubes may vary with tasks or commands that are appropriate to the level of readiness of the group. Cubes may also be constructed with tasks in a particular area of the multiple intelligences, such as verbal/linguistic, bodily/kinesthetic, or intrapersonal intelligence.

Why Do We Use Cubes?

Cubing, with its many sides, allows students to look at an issue or topic from a variety of angles and to develop a multidimensional perspective rather than a single one.

Cubes offer a chance to differentiate learning by readiness (familiarity with content or level of skill), student interest, and/or learning profile (multiple intelligences). Cubes may vary in color and tasks depending on the abilities and interests of the small group. They add an element of novelty and fun to the learning by providing uniqueness to the lesson. It is a great strategy for tactile/kinesthetic learners as they reinforce understanding and extend or demonstrate learning.

How Do We Use Cubes?

1. Keep clear learning goals in mind when considering the use of cubing for different learners.

2. Provide extended opportunities, materials, and learning situations that are appropriate for a wide range of readiness, interests, and learning styles.

3. Make sure students understand the verbs and directions for the tasks.

4. Group students according to readiness, with different colored cubes giving tasks or questions appropriate to their levels of understanding and ability in that particular topic or skill. Students assist one another in their learning.

5. Ask students to share findings with the large group or to form base groups of experts to share their tasks.

Figure 43 suggests verbs that may be used on all six sides of a cube.

Figure 43.   Use of Different Verbs, Tasks, and Commands on Each Side of a Cube

Cubing . . . Levels of Thinking

1. Tell Describe Recall Name Locate List	4. Review Discuss Prepare Diagram Cartoon
2. Compare Contrast Example Explain Define Write	5. Propose Suggest Finish Prescribe Devise
3. Connect Make Design Produce Develop	6. Debate Formulate Choose Support In your opinion . . .

Cubing may also be differentiated using multiple intelligences. Cubes may be designed with a variety of multiple intelligences activities to give students a chance to use their varied strengths. As an alternative, teachers can also use a die with numbers 1 to 6 and provide students with activity cards at various levels of complexity related to the topic (see Figure 44).

If students are studying the planets, for example, they might have a variety of cubes in the different multiple intelligences to process information for musical/rhythmic intelligence, bodily/kinesthetic intelligence, visual/spatial intelligence, and naturalist, logical/ mathematical, interpersonal, or intrapersonal intelligences. Or in a class where students are reading *Charlotte's Web*, by E. B. White, cubes could be used to deal with visual/spatial intelligence, and students could be given the following statements on the sides of their cubes.

Green Cube

1. Draw Charlotte as you think she looks.

2. Use a Venn diagram and compare Charlotte and Fern.

3. Use a comic strip to tell what happened in this chapter.

Figure 44.   Cubes Vary in Color and Tasks Depending on the
Prior Knowledge and Interests of the Learners

Green Cube	Blue Cube
1.	1.
2.	2.
3.	3.
4.	4.
5.	5.
6.	6.
Yellow Cube	Red Cube
1.	1.
2.	2.
3.	3.
4.	4.
5.	5.
6.	6.

4. Shut your eyes and describe the barn. Jot down your ideas.

5. Predict what will happen in the next chapter. Use symbols.

6. In your opinion, why is Charlotte a good friend?

Yellow Cube

1. Use a graphics program on the computer and create a character web for Wilbur.

2. Use symbols on a Venn diagram to compare Wilbur and Charlotte.

3. Use a storyboard to show the progress of the plot to this point.

4. Draw the farm and label the items, people, and buildings.

5. What is the message that you think the writer wants people to remember?

6. Draw a symbol that illustrates your idea.

7. When you think of the title, do you agree or disagree that it is a good choice? Why or why not?

Both cubes are tapping into using visual/spatial intelligence, with the green cube working at a more basic level, with key aspects of the story, and the yellow cube stretching student thinking more in the abstraction, extending ideas and making connections.

ROLE-PLAYING

What Is It?

Role-playing is when a student takes on the role of a character, perhaps from a story, play, or novel; a historical or political figure; or someone depicting a particular scenario that deals with a concern or issue such as conflict resolution.

Why Do We Do It?

Role-playing allows students to process knowledge and demonstrate skills in an emotionally laden context. It is a form of elaborative rehearsal that causes students to interact with content and concepts and, ideally, create an episodic memory. It affords students the opportunity to examine and organize information, deal with issues, and create or re-create situations that have meaning. The roles students take on allow them to become immersed in situations. They become that person or character and take on that persona. As they play that role, their emotions are involved, and the emotional brain punctuates the moment. Role-playing allows students to be involved at their levels. Many students have strong verbal and interpersonal skills, and this technique allows them to use those skills.

How Do We Do It?

Allow students the opportunity to be involved when they are comfortable. Encourage students to choose the type of role-playing they would like to do. Try using a "choice board" similar to the one shown in Figure 45. Teachers find that they must work within the comfort zones of students, as those who are more intrapersonal do not always embrace this technique because they may not be as gregarious as other students. Initially, teachers may have students engage in improvisation. As teachers begin to introduce this technique to students, they may want to use mime initially or provide a script. After several tries at role-playing, students may begin to write scripts for themselves. Props and scenery may be included if needed or available.

Figure 45.   Choice Board for Role-Playing

Directions: Choose one from each column for your role-playing project.

Format	Scenes	Props
Narrative actors	Transparencies	Artifacts
Interviews	Stage	Television frames
Mimes	Mural	Costumes

All students will need to identify appropriate audience interaction and behavior and monitor that behavior in role-playing situations. Feedback to participants should be positive and constructive. Reflection and emotional reactions should be processed after each attempt at role-playing. Role-playing places information and key concepts in a contextual learning situation and increases the chances for understanding and retention.

Teachers who use a variety of instructional strategies add novelty, choice, and individuality to the learning. These strategies allow diverse learners to find a size that fits and suits and to engage in practice and rehearsal to deepen understanding through as many learning styles and multiple intelligences as they can.

There are numerous instructional strategies, and we continue to learn and add to our expertise, like adding clothes to our wardrobes. However, as teachers build and increase their repertoires, they will see how they can adjust the learning for the group of learners and how different strategies appeal to different learners.

One size doesn't fit all, and, happily, one size doesn't have to.

Chapter 6 Reflections

1. Considering the "Best Practice, Brain Research" chart, Figure 30, which strategies are you using on a routine basis?

2. Which instructional strategy will you incorporate into your repertoire in the next month?

3. How will you do that? With what content might you try it?

4. With whom could you work and plan for this implementation?

5. How will you monitor student improvement or reaction to the use of this strategy?

CURRICULUM APPROACHES FOR DIFFERENTIATED CLASSROOMS 7

INDIVIDUAL ITEMS OF CLOTHING ARE PUT TOGETHER TO FORM a wardrobe. Wardrobes evolve and build over time as we add and discard articles. A variety of instructional tools develop and, when used strategically, are powerful in a differentiated classroom. The tools can be built into various curriculum approaches. The curriculum can be delivered in many ways so it will appeal to individual learners and their needs for novelty, engaging activities, and quests for meaning. In this chapter, we explore centers, projects, problem-based learning, inquiry, and contracts.

One way to organize the curriculum is to use centers or stations.

CENTERS

What Are They?

A *center* is a collection of material designed purposely with a goal in mind.

Students work with center materials to develop, discover, create, and learn a task at their own pace. Students are responsible for their learning during center time. There is always an established purpose for each center.

The hands-on experiences in centers provide opportunities for learners to

- Remediate, enhance, or extend knowledge on a skill, concept, standard, or topic
- Pursue interests and explore the world of knowledge
- Work at the level of need and be challenged
- Be creative and critical problem solvers
- Make choices, establish their own pace, and build persistence
- Manipulate a variety of different types of materials
- Facilitate complex thinking and dendritic growth

Centers are an ideal design for adjustable assignments. Centers can be set up in different ways:

- A variety of centers on a topic or theme in a particular subject area with different levels of difficulty
- Interest centers for further investigation of a topic
- Free-inventing centers for experimenting, discovering, and inventing
- Computer centers with multimedia resources for supplemental or remedial use

- Resource centers with a wide variety of reading materials
- Art media table to create artifacts that represent learning and creativity
- Role-playing centers to demonstrate characters and sequence of events
- Manipulatives centers for hands-on learning
- Skills centers for adjustable assignments
- Writing centers with a variety of writing tools and various types and sizes of paper
- Challenge centers for problem solving
- Listening centers with music or reading with both fictional and factual content
- Multiple intelligences centers that provide students with choices related to the topic

A structured center has specific tasks assigned and an agenda developed by the teacher. During center time, students work with skills or concepts, approaching them through a variety of experiences. Multilevel tasks are often designed for a certain skill or objective for this type of center. During center time, students work at their levels of need and at their own pace, while being challenged with complex, hands-on learning (see also Chapman & Freeman, 1996).

An exploratory center has materials provided and allows the student to decide what to do with those materials. For example, a reading nook is available with a wide variety of different types of reading materials. The student decides which material to read and how long to read. A student settles down to read a selection because of a high interest in the topic and an appropriate reading level (see also Chapman & Freeman, 1996).

Establishing centers facilitates many diverse opportunities for learning to take place. The teacher can consciously adjust activities for the centers in the planning process and assign appropriate learners to the various centers. Centers are places where the work can be made to fit the learner's needs, ranging from basic learning, to remediation, to enrichment. They set up opportunities for understanding a skill or a concept through a variety of experiences. By having a variety of materials and tasks at one station, students become more responsible for their learning. They make their own choices and set individualized goals. There is an intrinsic reward for self-achievement. Centers provide opportunities to pursue individual interests and talents with greater immersion in the topic.

How Do We Use Them?
Choice Centers

Secondary history teacher Diane Huggler (Corning, NY) set up "Ancient Civilization Learning Centers," which included the students' choices of China, Japan, Africa, the Middle East, Southwest Asia, and the Pacific.

The Goal. Your group's task is to discover as much about your civilization as you can from a variety of sources and present the information to the class.

The Procedure

- Each group has a set of color-coded folders that explain criteria for this task and help you discover information about your ancient peoples.

- Each person in the group will have a certain role within the group to make sure that it functions smoothly and completes its task successfully.
- Class time is to be used to complete the folder activities. Record your progress in the group log/journal.

The Presentation

- You will become the experts on your civilization and have the opportunity to share your knowledge with your classmates.
- Your group needs to prepare a PowerPoint presentation, with each group member being responsible for at least two slides.
- You may also use other teaching tools, such as the overhead projector, the chalkboard, maps, pictures, and so on, to tap the multiple intelligences.
- Your presentation needs to be at least 15 minutes long, and you need to be prepared to answer classmates' questions.

The Grade

- You will be assessed in three areas using a rubric that identifies how well you performed in the following categories:

1. Content

    2   4   6   8

2. Presentation

    2   4   6   8

3. Group skills

    2   4   6   8

4. Individual contributions

    2   4   6   8

Math Rotation Centers

Another scenario is the creation of "Math Rotation Centers." Students work in each center to complete all tasks. They sign into centers the day before and keep track on their agendas.

Center 1. *Stock Update:* At this center, students are involved in a simulation of creating their own stock portfolios, such that they buy and sell stocks and keep track of the profits or losses.

Students are directed to complete the first update sheet in their stock folders, identifying profits or losses. They use information online or in the newspapers provided.

Center 2. *Folder Check:* At this center, students examine and organize their math portfolios. Portfolios should include notes, mental math papers, reflections, and mind maps of solutions, followed by all graded papers with corrections. Be sure the reflection is attached. When students finish their folders, they may move on to . . . the "BIG ONE" and "Fraction Card Game": This center involves students playing games with others in groups with the same-color folders. The key concept is identifying equivalent fractions. Games may be played only after all players have completed their folder checks.

Center 3. Changing Fractions to Decimals: This center uses Versa Tiles to self-correct activities. These tasks involve a basic understanding of finding equivalent fractions and decimals as well as an introduction to ratios.

Center 4. Chocolate Delight: At this center, students take an 8½" × 11" sheet of paper and fold it in half, as per the instructions. After renaming the equivalent fractions, students are asked to write the explanation on the back of half the paper. Then they proceed to the self-correcting worksheets using a dry-erase marker, and erase all answers when finished.

Differentiating Within a Center

When preparing differentiated activities for a center, it can be helpful to work with the three levels of the adjustable-assignments grid: *Beginning Mastery, Approaching Mastery,* and *High Degree of Mastery.* Depending on their mastery levels, students may be discovering, exploring, enhancing, or practicing the current information being taught; reviewing the information that has been taught; or exploring an upcoming topic.

Today's students play video and computer games with levels, so they are accustomed to this method. Center activity assignments can be color coded and labeled, for example:

Beginning Mastery	Level 1: Green
Approaching Mastery	Level 2: Yellow
High Degree of Mastery	Level 3: Purple

When a student goes to the center, he or she first works on the area of need. After the teacher assignment has been completed, the student can then work in an area of choice.

Thematic Centers: Experiments

The theme of these centers, adapted from versions used by the Halton Board of Education (Halton, Ontario), was "Eggs." The centers consisted of scientific experiments that were part of an integrated unit called "Great Eggspectations." The examples in Figures 46 and 47 show the planning for two of the centers, paying attention to

- Standards and content
- Who will be working in the center
- Activities
- Materials needed
- Location
- Assessment
- Teacher reflections

Figure 48 shows a template that may be used to plan centers.

Figure 46.   Center Example: The Magic Egg

Center: The Magic Egg

Standards: Recognize changes in matter

Content: To demonstrate the semipermeability of a cell membrane. The shell is affected by vinegar and carbon dioxide forms. The membrane will turn rubbery. The egg will swell because the contents of the egg cannot pass through the tiny holes in the membrane. The water in the vinegar passes through the membrane into the egg and causes it to swell.

Who: Group of 4, heterogeneous group

Activities	Materials
Small group: 1. Measure around the center of the egg and record. 2. Describe the egg. 3. Place the egg in the jar. Do not break the shell. 4. Cover the egg with vinegar. 5. Close the lid. 6. Look at it right away and then look at it at different times for the next 3 days. 7. Remove the egg after 3 days and measure once again around its middle. 8. Compare what the egg looks like now and before it was in the vinegar.	• 1 raw egg • 1 jar with a lid (the egg must fit in the jar) • Clear vinegar • Measuring tape that is flexible
	Location
	Table in corner of room by the window. Roles for group members: 1. Recorder 2. Materials handler 3. Reader and reporter

Assessment	Teacher Reflections
Predictions. Group booklet will be produced containing recordings of the experiments. Cooperative skills reflection.	

SOURCE: Used with permission from the Halton Board of Education (Halton, Ontario).

Figure 47.   Center Example: Bottled Eggs

Center: Bottled Eggs

Standards: To develop scientific principles of experimentation. To develop the skills of hypothesis, inference, and prediction; problem solving; and decision making.

Content: To determine a way in which one can fit a hard-boiled egg through a small-necked bottle without breaking it.

Who: Group of 4, heterogeneous group

Activities	Materials
Teacher information: Hot water creates and leaves steam in the bottle and that forces out some air. When the steam changes to droplets of water, it doesn't need as much space. So the air pressure is reduced and the pressure of the air outside the bottle forces the egg into the bottle.	• A hard-boiled egg, peeled • A small-necked jar (slightly smaller than the egg) • Boiling water

	Location
Directions for group: 1. Pour boiling water into the bottle. 2. Shake it around and then pour it out. 3. Place the egg over the mouth of the bottle. 4. Record your observations. 5. To remove the egg, turn the bottle upside down, and place your mouth over the opening and blow into it for about half a minute.	Small group by table near the sink. Roles for group members: • Recorder, reporter • Materials manager • Encourager (reader)

Assessment	Teacher Reflections
Were the students successful in placing the egg in and out of the bottle? Group log and findings Group reflection	

SOURCE: Used with permission from the Halton Board of Education (Halton, Ontario).

Figure 48. Center Planning Template

Center:

Standards: _____

Content: _____

_____

_____

Who: _____

Activities	Materials
	Location
Assessment	**Teacher Reflections**

Management Techniques

Establish clearly defined, effective workspaces for centers. They might be a desktop, a carpet square, a lab station, a table, or a corner of the room. They are spaces for working with a particular set of materials related to particular tasks.

When setting up the centers, be sure to label the materials. For instance, if certain pieces go with one task, color code or put a symbol on them to coordinate them as a set to enable quick identification. Also give them a "home" so they can be found and returned to the same location. This way, the materials are organized and labeled properly for easy access. Students need to assist in the distribution and cleaning up of materials. Design a system that is easy and efficient. Consider the uniqueness of the situation and plan accordingly. It is better to prethink management strategies than to have things go "off the rails" and thus waste valuable learning time while you rethink logistics.

Establish and teach rules so that all participants have a common understanding. Many times, the expectations for the regular classroom will also cover center work.

For example, "Work quietly and respect others" is as relevant in centers as anywhere in the classroom.

Establish a common signal to get students' attention so all the students know what the signal is and what to do when they hear it. This is valuable when directions need to be given to a large group or when it is time to clean up.

Sometimes, students finish their work at a center before the time for center work is finished. That is when focus or sponge activities come into play. There should always be something meaningful and productive to do next. Often, it can be a reflection or journal or log entry or another form of student self-assessment.

At times, the teacher is stationed in a center. Students rotate and come to the teacher's table to work. This works well when the teacher needs to give special attention to a particular group. The students at the other centers learn to self-monitor and become self-directed learners.

When centers have been set up based on interests or when students use them for sponge activities, they can eventually lose their appeal. At this point, the teacher should introduce a new interest center based on his or her observations and assessment of students' needs and preferences.

Students are often allowed to go to a new center of interest if time permits. Teacher monitoring and conferencing about quality work will mediate the decision to move on to a new center.

How Do We Assess?

One way to discover the thinking processes that students use when approaching tasks or problems is assessing center time. When asked the appropriate questions, students make their thinking known to the teacher. Assessment shows whether or where students have difficulties and which parts they understand and which need clarification. Proper assistance and follow-up can then be given to keep the students learning at their own rates toward the targeted standards.

Assessment during center time is essential. Students and teachers continue to dialogue, to give and receive feedback. Teachers who ask the right questions during this time can learn so much about their students. When open-ended questions are asked, students reflect on their thinking and explain their processes. Expressing orally how they solved that particular problem or accomplished a task lets students become more metacognitive and reflective about their tasks. Using anecdotal note taking or an observation checklist along with effective questions, teachers begin to understand where the students are in their learning/thinking and often where they need to go next. Assessment should inform practice and tell us how students are progressing and what adjustments should be made to a program.

Both the students and the teacher should pay attention to assessment data to inform the next steps.

Teacher Assessment Strategies

Teachers move in and out of the centers to interact with the learners and monitor their progress. Ongoing conferencing keeps learners on task and gives teachers the data necessary to adjust or change any activities that are not challenging enough or perhaps are too challenging. Ongoing modification is often necessary to adjust tasks when there is a need to do so.

Anecdotal Finding. Teachers often record anecdotal findings of observations for record-keeping purposes.

Some teachers refer to this as "clipboard cruising" (see Figure 49). The data collection sheet may look something like the one in Figure 49, with columns for note taking.

Figure 49.   Clipboard Cruising for Data Collection

Clipboard Cruising

Name	Date	Time	Center or Task	Observed Behavior
_____	_____	_____	_____	_____
_____	_____	_____	_____	_____
_____	_____	_____	_____	_____
_____	_____	_____	_____	_____
_____	_____	_____	_____	_____
_____	_____	_____	_____	_____
_____	_____	_____	_____	_____

Checklists. Use a checklist to assess the behaviors being observed. Teachers observing center time design the most effective checklists because they are familiar with the information and its location on the list. It should take longer to develop the checklist than to score it. The teacher who will be using it designs the most effective checklist; each item fits a particular situation. Also, if the person who made the checklist is the one scoring it, that person is familiar with the data and it is easy to use.

Center time checklists (see Figure 50) should address the targeted needs of the group. One list could address social skills; another, time cognitive skills; and yet another, both. Figure 50 offers some sample observable behaviors to include in a checklist.

Effective Questioning Techniques

Open-Ended Questions and Statements. Have students demonstrate what they know by asking appropriate questions. The right questions get students to convey their thinking processes, which are unique to how each student approaches a task or problem at a particular time. This evidence shows where there are weaknesses and strengths, misunderstandings or clarity.

The following are some examples of effective questions:

- Tell me what you are doing.
- How did you do that?
- Tell me step-by-step how you made that.

Student Self-Assessment

Students can use log and journal entries for self-assessment. Some suggestions for logs or journals include the following:

a. Today, I want to tell you _____. Choose one of the following that you would like to share:
 - What I am doing
 - Why I am doing it
 - Why it is important
 - How I can use it
 - Why I chose to do this
 - What I need next

b. Four Thoughts Feedback
 - The part I like best is _____.
 - The part I am not clear about is _____.
 - Someone needs to tell me more about _____.
 - Next time, I need to _____.

c. Today, I will receive the _____ award. Make an award certificate or ribbon.

Centers themselves can be assessed by students after they have worked in them. Cards may be placed at the centers for students to give their feedback to the teacher (see Figure 51). You may want to include some or all of the information in Figure 51.

Figure 50. Center Checklists: Used to Address Targeted Needs of the Group

Center Checklist

Name _____   Center _____   Unit of Study _____

Type of Assignment _____ Assigned _____ Student Choice _____

Teacher   Date _____ Signature _____

Peer   Date _____ Signature _____

Self   Date _____ Signature _____

Work Habits	*Not Yet*	*Sometimes*	*Most of the Time*
Stays on task			
Gets work done on time			
Uses materials appropriately			
Completes tasks			
Follows rules at the center			
Uses time wisely			

Social Skills

Shares materials

Listens to others

Helps others

Respects self and others

Shows patience

Group work

Takes turns

Shares materials and ideas

Participates appropriately

Focuses on one person talking

Communicates appropriately

Works well with others

Helps others

COMMENTS:

Figure 51.   Sample Feedback Card for Students
                  to Assess Centers After They Have Worked in Them

Name _____ Center _____ Date _____

At this center I learned _____

_____

_____

Centers that I worked in today were

1. _____

2. _____

While I was there I _____

How would you rate your learning?

1   2   3   4   5   Wow

Journal entries are also useful after center work. Here are a few suggestions for journal stems that help students reflect on their work:

- The best thing about this center time was _____.

- The worst thing about this center time was _____.

- Next time, I _____.

- I learned _____.

- This is what I did, step-by-step: _____.

Center time can be some of the most productive time in the classroom. When the centers are set up with thoughtful, challenging materials that develop students' learning, they offer meaningful learning experiences in which students learn and explore. Centers should not be just for fun experiences or time fillers, but for learning experiences based on targeted standards that are designed to meet the needs of a variety of different learners. They are also great vehicles for offering students opportunities to use their various multiple intelligences. Figure 52, "Multiple Intelligences: Suggestions for Centers and Projects," gives ample suggestions for centers and projects.

Figure 52.   Multiple Intelligences: Suggestions for Centers and Projects

Verbal/Linguistic
Prepare a report.
Write a play or essay.
Create a poem or recitation.
Listen to an audiotape on . . .
Interview.
Label a diagram.
Give directions for . . .

Bodily/Kinesthetic
Create a role-play.
Construct a model or representation.
Develop a mime.
Create a tableau for . . .
Manipulate materials.
Work through a simulation.
Create actions for . . .

Musical/Rhythmic
Compose a rap song or rhyme.
Create a jingle to teach others.
Listen to musical selections about . . .
Write a poem.
Select music or songs for a particular
   purpose.

Naturalist
Discover or experiment.
Categorize materials or ideas.
Look for ideas from nature.
Adapt materials to a new use.
Connect ideas to nature.
Examine materials to make generalizations.

Visual/Spatial
Draw a picture.
Create a mural or display.
Illustrate an event.
Make a diagram.
Create a cartoon.
Paint or design a poster.
Design a graphic.
Use color to . . .

Interpersonal
Work with a partner or group.
Discuss and come to conclusions.
Solve a problem together.
Survey or interview others.
Dialogue about a topic.
Use cooperative groups.

Logical/Mathematical
Create a pattern.
Describe a sequence or process.
Develop a rationale.
Analyze a situation.
Critically assess . . .
Classify, rank, or compare . . .
Interpret evidence . . .
Timeline.

Intrapersonal
Think about and plan.
Write in a journal.
Review or visualize a way to do
   something.
Make a connection with past information
   or experiences.
Metacognitive moment.

PROJECTS FOR DIFFERENTIATED CLASSROOMS

What Are They?

A project is an in-depth study. Students explore a topic as investigators, researchers, and discoverers of knowledge. Projects can be varied and rich with opportunities for engaging learners and for deep understanding at a variety of levels of readiness, interests, or learning profiles. Projects are usually in a certain subject area dealing with a particular topic of study.

Projects can be assigned or chosen from a choice list or board. When deciding on a selection from the list, make sure each choice meets certain criteria:

- Is age appropriate so the students can do the assignment independently
- Teaches content being taught during the year
- Provides choices
- Fits an established timeline
- Is assessed by the established assessment tool

Structured Projects

In structured projects, the expectations and guidelines are structured and are shared with the students. Students work creatively to achieve success, given their understanding of concepts and the skills they have mastered. For example, in Geometry, students are assigned the "Building Project" (build the tallest structure that will stand alone using the materials given). The project may be assigned to the whole class but responded to individually or in small groups.

Topic-Related Projects

These projects are typical, traditional school projects. Students choose a topic that interests and motivates them and produce a product that shows what has been learned or what is particularly significant to the learners. For example, students may choose a political figure, an issue, or a particular place or event associated with World War II that interests them.

Open-Ended Projects

These projects have minimal guidelines and few criteria and are loosely structured, to encourage risk taking and creativity. These projects may be a challenge that causes students to draw on their knowledge and skills to produce a product that addresses the challenge. One middle school class looked at developing innovative products that would be useful to the elderly. The unit contained literacy skills as students developed questionnaires, surveys, and interviews to gather data from the elderly. They used the Internet to access information on trends and needs. They used principles of simple machines and other science and math skills. In a hands-on and creative component, they designed their inventions.

Why Do We Use Them?

Projects are used because they build on students' interest and satisfy curiosity. Students learn to plan their time and develop their research skills at various levels. Projects provide students with choices, ownership, and responsibility. They encourage independence and self-directed learning skills and allow students to work at complex and abstract levels that match their skill levels while managing time and materials. Projects are highly motivating and allow for in-depth work on interesting topics. Projects allow students to work at their own rates. However, they must be worth the academic time of the learner and be meaningful experiences, not just time fillers. Projects help the learner to interact with knowledge at a level higher than simple recall. They also help develop concepts more fully and enable students to construct their own understanding. Information learned in context with an emotional hook will be remembered longer if it is also a meaningful experience. Projects emphasize process as well as product and integrate many concepts, facts, and skills.

How Do We Use Them?

All projects need to be designed with the end in mind. That means the project is designed based on clear learning goals, standards, and content objectives. Projects should be age appropriate and at the students' levels so the work is interesting and challenging without being overwhelming.

Teachers usually provide students with a suggestion list for projects. Design the list with a variety of intelligences targeted both so that the learners can work on an area of strength for the presentation and format and because students' learning styles are diverse (see Figure 15 in Chapter 3, "Suggestions for Using the Eight Multiple Intelligences," and Figure 52, "Multiple Intelligences: Suggestions for Centers and Projects," earlier in this chapter). This allows learners to concentrate on information and spend time on developing comprehension and a deeper understanding of the topic rather than always having to use verbal/linguistic models like essays, research papers, or oral presentations.

Procedure for Project Work

1. Choose a topic.

2. Develop a plan of action that includes a timeline, a distribution of duties if working in a group, and so on.

3. Implement the plan.

   Gather ideas
   List resources
   Decide on the format
   Refer to a rubric
   Conference
   Compile ideas
   Prepare presentation

4. Display and presentation.

Evaluation: Self, Peer, Teacher, Significant Other

Students may be given the option to submit a contract for a project. This contract should meet the same criteria as the other suggested project assignments but would reflect the area of study chosen by the student. The student presents the contract to the teacher for approval. This is done best in a teacher/student conference so the learner can explain his or her thinking and ideas in detail. The teacher negotiates with the student until a reasonable contract is completed. Contracts may be proposed because the student has an interest in learning more about a particular area. This is important to learning because it satisfies the learner's personal learning needs. Students with a keen need and desire to learn will indeed learn more. They will be more committed and engaged and will invest more time and energy in the project.

Assessment

Rubrics are designed with clear criteria and indicators to establish expectations and the grading format. They include a detailed explanation of the requirements. Students should be clear up front about the criteria for success, and the rubric can guide them as they work on the project. The rubric informs the teacher, the student, and the parents about the requirements, guidelines, and expectations for the project from the beginning to the end (see Figure 53).

Students log and journal their timelines, findings, and procedures to show what they are learning, using, and processing. If working with others, they need to negotiate the workload and facilitate the project by using appropriate social skills. Students also need to reflect on the group's interactions as they work together. Teachers assign or students select the roles and duties for which they will be accountable.

Adjustable Projects

The teacher provides a range of resources matching the readiness levels of the students. The materials should be multilevel and age appropriate. Adequate time must be spent on gathering and selecting the resources. Students select resources suitable for their projects and naturally select materials that are appropriate to their readiness levels. Learners rarely choose materials that they can't read or understand. Thus projects are invariably adjusted as a matter of course because of the individuality of each student. A variety of multimedia and human resources can also be used for project work. The Internet and technology are valuable tools and should be considered for project work. They are intriguing and engaging for many learners and help develop the skills of accessing, gathering, and managing information.

Sample Projects
Integer Project

Math teacher Ellen Wilken (Granville, OH), who wanted her students to really understand integers, designed the following project choices.

Demonstrate knowledge of integer operations (+, –, =, ×) by using one of the following projects:

1. Make an 8½" × 11" chart showing integer operation rules with examples.

2. Write a poem, newspaper article, or comic strip about integers.

3. Construct a three-dimensional art object, puzzle, or game that uses integer computation.

4. Write and perform a live or videotaped play.

5. Write and perform a song or jingle.

6. Interview someone outside the class about that person's understanding of integers. Record or videotape the responses.

Figure 53. Rubric for Project

Name _____

Project _____

Date _____

Self _____

Peer _____

Teacher _____

Accuracy of Information

2 _____ 3 _____ 4 _____ 5

Use of Visuals

2 _____ 3 _____ 4 _____ 5

Completion

2 _____ 3 _____ 4 _____ 5

Presentation

2 _____ 3 _____ 4 _____ 5

Team Member Involvement

2 _____ 3 _____ 4 _____ 5

Used Time Appropriately

2 _____ 3 _____ 4 _____ 5

Comments:

7. Write an autobiography about your understanding of integer computation and how it will help you in future situations.

8. Show evidence of integers in nature by use of photography, samples, or drawings.

She reported that students were highly engaged as they worked on their choices alone or with a partner. They had a far greater understanding and ability to apply that understanding as a result of the project work.

Nutrition and Wellness Project

The following is an example of nutrition project choices that teacher Cindy Palur (Granville, OH) designed to consciously offer options in the area of multiple intelligences.

Action Project Ideas for Nutrition Class

If you are musical or rhythmic, you might like to

- Compose a song related to wellness
- Create a nutritional poem
- Make up a health-related rap song

If you like to write or talk, you might like to

- Write memos to be announced each morning to improve student wellness
- Create a nutritional commercial
- Write a report related to a wellness issue
- Create a nutritional brochure
- Read a nutritional or health-related book and make a report
- Interview a health professional and report your findings
- Keep a daily journal of your eating and exercise for a week and report on how they can be improved

If you like to dance or perform, you might like to

- Perform a play, dance, or skit depicting various elements of nutrition (eating disorders, coronary disease, etc.)
- Make a complete dinner for friends or family
- Create a routine or jazzercise dance to your favorite song and teach it to several friends
- Compose a poem or make a tape or video of an element related to wellness

If you like to work with others, you might like to

- Volunteer at a food pantry or soup kitchen
- Volunteer to help a caterer
- Survey people who work in some aspect of nutrition and help them make positive changes to improve their levels of wellness. Keep in touch as to their progress (e.g., set up an exercise or low-fat eating program)
- Organize an exercise or workout group and meet regularly
- Teach an elementary class an aspect of nutrition (e.g., "5 a Day")

If you like to use numbers or graphs or solve abstract problems, you might like to

- Collect data to make a graph to show the relationship of a health issue (e.g., Is there a relationship between students who eat five fruits and vegetables a day and normal weight?)
- Develop a board game
- Do a science experiment related to food (amount of fat, sugar, salt, acid base, etc.)
- Determine how many calories you need each day based on your size and level of activity and create a menu to reflect that number of calories
- Use a computer to create a nutritional or health brochure
- Compare and contrast various nutritional information (e.g., water versus sports drinks)
- Do research related to food

If you like independent study and self-improvement, you might like to

- Keep a diary of your diet for a week and determine ways you can improve to meet the requirements of the Food Pyramid and Dietary Guidelines
- Plan family meals for a week and create a shopping list
- Set wellness goals and ways to accomplish them (e.g., gain weight, lose weight, or exercise regularly) and keep track of your progress
- Attend a wellness conference, seminar, or workshop and report your findings

If you like to draw or create, you might like to

- Draw a picture or poster depicting good nutrition for display in the cafeteria
- Create a new recipe and test it on friends or family
- Create an educational game around aspects of wellness or good nutrition
- Make a videotape showing good nutritional ideas
- Create new garnish ideas using food to entice young eaters to try new foods
- Draw an artistic wellness brochure

If you are interested in nature and growing things, you might like to

- Grow your own food and use it in a recipe (e.g., herbs)
- Freeze, can, dry, or preserve food for later use (frozen corn, canned tomatoes, applesauce, jelly, frozen broccoli, dried apples, etc.)

Animal Project

Here is another example of project choices, created by a Chicago teacher, Jamie Downhower.

Your job is to teach the kindergarten and first-grade classes all about your animal. You are going to show them your trading card of your animal. You are also going to need to choose one of the items from below to create to put on display for our classroom zoo.

- Use a box to create a habitat that looks like the environment where your animal lives.
- Write a journal pretending that you are an animal expert who is observing your animal in the wild for a week. Be sure to write about what it does all day long.

- Pretend your animal is being taken to a country where no one has ever seen that kind of animal before. Write a newspaper article telling all about it; be sure to include information about what it eats, what it looks like, its size, its natural habitat, and so on.

- Write a story or a poem featuring your animal.

- Create a magazine advertisement encouraging people to donate money to help bring your animal to the Lincoln Park Zoo.

- Make a brochure educating people on all of the interesting facts about your animal.

- Make a life-sized picture of your animal, with lots of detail.

- Create a poster with important information about your animal.

- Draw a comic book featuring your animal.

- Design a map of the world and show where your animal is originally from.

- Create a papier-mâché model of your animal.

- Make a pop-up book with your animal as the star.

- Create a food chain showing which animals eat your animal and which animals your animal eats.

- Write a letter to your state representatives telling them why your animal is important and ask them to help take care of it.

- If you have a different idea, please ask me about it before you get started.

Migration Project

A variation of the animal project was used by Drew Tessler and Jamie Downhower, of Chicago, to create a Migration Project (see Figure 54).

Social Studies Project on the Bill of Rights

Social studies teacher Keisha Gabriel, from High Point Central High School in North Carolina, used multiple intelligences when designing a unit about the Bill of Rights. She created a "choice board" for students to choose activities to demonstrate knowledge (see Figure 55).

Solar System Project

Here is an example of a choice board that Jamie Downhower created for his class in Chicago Public Schools for his unit on the Solar System (see Figure 56).

Figure 54.   Sample Choice Board for Migration Project

Name _____ Date _____

Menu for Migration: Your job is to complete four activities this week—one from each box.

1.
A. What are the different things that we need to live? Draw a picture for each thing and write about why each is so important.
B. Create a Venn diagram (with two circles) to compare Ancient Peoples (Ancient Romans, Vikings, Earliest Americans, or other Ancient Peoples you have studied) to the modern lives that we have now.
	2.
	A. Find a partner and draw out the migration routes on the maps. Label these areas:
	    Canada
	    United States
	    North America
	    South America
	    Mexico
	    Atlantic, Pacific, and Arctic Oceans

3.
A. Imagine: A lot of your friends have gone across the Land Bridge.
Write a letter to your family persuading them to move to one of the areas below.
Let them know why you want to move.
What are your reasons for going across to a new continent?
Include a postcard of what life would be like from that place.
Choices:
    Arctic
    Mountains
    Seaside
    Tropical
    Plains
    Forests
    Around Lake Michigan
***Remember: Things won't look like they do now! This is over 10,000 years ago!
	4.
	A. You are in Chicago, and you are going to move to the desert during the summer. What would you need to live comfortably in the desert and to survive? Make a list and draw pictures of the items that you will need.
	B. Write a short story where you are one of the first people on this continent. What is it like moving to a new place? What kinds of changes do you need to be ready for? Why choose one place over another? What hardships have you gone through to get to where you wanted to go?

SOURCE: Created by Drew Tessler and Jamie Downhower, Chicago.

Figure 55.   Bill of Rights Choice Board

Interpersonal	Intrapersonal	Visual/Spatial
Create a Bill of Rights for your school	Journal: Explain how you use the First Amendment freedoms on a daily basis.	Video: *School House Rocks* Create a poster for each amendment with newspaper articles.
Bodily/Kinesthetic Role-Play: Constitutional Convention	**Wild Card!**	**Naturalist** Several scenarios of rights taken away. Student identifies which right and which amendment was in question.
Logical/Mathematical Timeline of events leading to the Constitution	**Musical/Rhythmic** Create a rap, poem, or song for the Bill of Rights	**Verbal/Linguistic** Mnemonic on First Amendment—RAPPS: **R**eligion, **A**ssembly, **P**etition, **P**ress, **S**peech

Figure 56.   Choice Board for Studying the Solar System

Science: Solar System: Study of the Planets

MUST DO:

Using the research sites bookmarked on our classroom computer, please choose one planet and use Kidspiration to prewrite an expository essay about what your planet looks like, how big it is, and what kind of gases are found on your planet. Please include lots of interesting facts you have learned from your research.

DO:

Use Kidspiration to create a word map. Include 12 facts: one about each planet and three other interesting facts about the solar system. Be sure to include pictures as well.

Write three specific questions about space that will later be e-mailed by the teacher to an astronaut at NASA.	Compare and contrast your planet with planet Earth. If your planet is Earth, choose any other planet to make your comparison.	Pretend you are an astronaut and write a diary entry to family on Earth about your day in space. Include what kind of experiments you did, what you ate, and where you slept.
Research the phases of the moon online and create a picture book with all of the phases and a one- or two-sentence summary of each phase. (Use the white paper by the project board to make your book.)	Your choice! Let's talk about it!	Pretend you are a travel agent and are creating a travel brochure for Chicago to attract visitors for all four seasons. Write about the kinds of weather that visitors can expect and draw lots of pictures to convince people to visit during each season.
Sketch your dream space shuttle. Please include as many details as possible and a paragraph describing your shuttle on the large paper near the project board.	Make a movie poster for a movie about space exploration. On the poster, include a drawing of the planets, sun, and moon.	Research constellations on the Internet or in one of our classroom books. Then create your own constellation using the star stickers on the project board. Write a story about how it was formed and why it is called by its name.

SOURCE: Adapted from Jamie Downhower, Chicago Public Schools.

CHOICE BOARDS

Choice boards give students multiple ways of processing information and rehearsing content and skills. Students may work alone and/or with one or more partners to accomplish the tasks they choose. Students may choose three in a row from a tic-tac-toe–style choice board and then make a free choice, or they may create their own tasks for a wild card. Choice boards can have multiple choice lines, shapes, formats, and options (see Figures 57–59), and they may also be organized around multiple intelligences (see Figure 60).

Figure 57.   Sample Choice Board for Social Studies

Each student signs up to join a group to work on an area of interest. Make sure there are more "choice lines" than students so that everyone gets to select a favorite area.

Today's Country _____

Government	Geography	Beliefs and Rituals
1. _____	1. _____	1. _____
2. _____	2. _____	2. _____
3. _____	3. _____	3. _____
4. _____	4. _____	4. _____

People	Recreation	Occupations
1. _____	1. _____	1. _____
2. _____	2. _____	2. _____
3. _____	3. _____	3. _____
4. _____	4. _____	4. _____

Figure 58.   Sample Choice Wheel

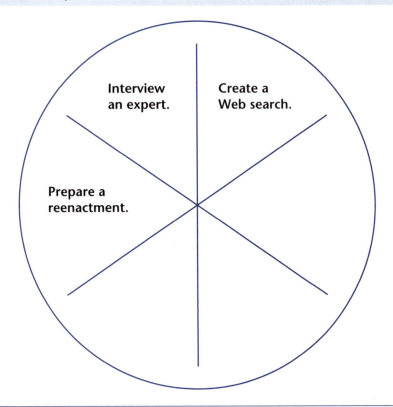

Figure 59.   Choice Boards May Include Scrolls and Pyramids

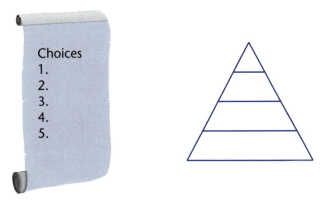

Figure 60. Multiple Intelligences Choice Board		
Verbal/Linguistic Prepare a report Write a play or essay Give directions for . . . Create a poem or recitation Listen to a tape or view a video Retell in your own words Create a word web	**Musical/Rhythmic** Create a rap, song, or ballad Write a jingle Write a poem Select music to enhance a story or event Create rhymes that . . .	**Visual/Spatial** Create a mural, poster, or drawing Illustrate an event Draw a diagram Design a graphic organizer Use color to . . . Create a comic strip to show . . . Do a story board Create a collage with meaningful artifacts
Logical/Mathematical Create a pattern Describe a sequence or process Develop a rationale Analyze a situation Create a sequel Critically assess. Classify, rank, or compare . . . Interpret evidence Design a game to show . . .	**Free Choice**	**Bodily/Kinesthetic** Create a role-play Construct a model or representation Develop a mime Create a tableau for . . . Manipulate materials to work through a simulation Create actions for . . .
Naturalist Discover or experiment Categorize materials or ideas Look for ideas from nature Adapt materials to a new use Connect ideas to nature Examine materials to make generalizations Label and classify Draw conclusions based on information Predict . . .	**Interpersonal** Work with a partner or group Discuss and come to conclusion Solve a problem together Survey or interview others Dialogue about a topic Use cooperative groups . . . to do a group project Project a character's point of view	**Intrapersonal** Think about and plan Write in a journal Keep track of . . . and comment on . . . Review or visualize a way Reflect on the character and express his or her feelings Image how it would feel if you . . .

PROBLEM-BASED LEARNING

What Is It?

Problem-based learning consists of providing students with ill-structured problems that are open-ended and challenging. Students use information and processes in real-world situations to solve the problems. Problem-based learning as a curriculum choice gives students the opportunity to work on problems in real-life scenarios. These problems are loosely structured and have no single right answer. They require investigation of options and application of the content and processes that students are studying and practicing.

Why Do It?

Howard Gardner (1993) defines *intelligence* as the ability to solve problems, handle crises, and produce something of value for one's culture. The ability to problem solve is an identified standard in most school districts. Students who learn only the facts may do well in a trivia game, but the ability to access information and use it practically and creatively (Sternberg, 1996) is a worthier goal because it is useful throughout life. Problem-based learning provides the brain with conditions that intrigue and engage. It allows for creative opportunities that provide learners with the chance to use their skills and capabilities in a variety of ways, use a range of resources, and balance their choices of learning with the teacher-directed objectives.

How Do We Do It?

Steps in Problem Solving

When students are solving problems, they must take the following steps:

- Clarify or identify the problem.
- Draw on background knowledge and experience.
- Begin with what you know.
- Plan your own approach.
- Work at your own pace.
- Use creative solutions.

Clarify the Problem

Through discussion and questioning, students identify the issues and discover the significant parts of the problem to address. A problem statement is then articulated.

Identify Resources

Students need to examine resources, including information and processes that they know from past experiences. KND is a chart that may be helpful for organizing this information (see Fogarty, 1998; Stepien, Gallagher, & Workman, 1993). The K stands for "What do you KNOW about this problem?" The N stands for "What do you NEED to solve this problem?" And the D stands for "What will you DO to get what you need?" Some teachers add a fourth element: P for PLAN. Students can often generate the first three columns but cannot get organized enough to proceed with their investigations. Planning is a step that many students need to think about. A plan may be modified as new ideas and information come up, but it serves to help students get started on their problem solving.

What do we Know? What do we Need to know? What can we Do? Beginning Plan?

Accessing Information

Once students identify what they need to know, they can generate sources for that information or process. This gives them opportunities to use the Internet and other information-accessing systems.

Generating Hypotheses

After all information is uncovered and collected, students generate hypotheses for solutions.

Selecting and Rationalizing Solutions

A solution that students think best fits the problem is presented with backup rationale.

Sometimes, teachers ask students to take on an authentic role in the problem and to present to a real audience. One teacher asked students to work in groups as travel agents to design a trip to their state capital. They were to highlight the historical/geographical features of the city/area and present their findings to parents with a rationale as to why the class should visit the capital. This problem engaged learners in various ways. They were motivated to take the trip and find out what would be interesting to visit and also to present that information to parents. The teacher had targeted the learning goals and then enticed the students to take ownership of the learning in a hands-on, practical way.

Secondary teacher Michael Bait asked the following of his physics students: "Construct an apparatus that can consistently project a steel ball to hit a target." He asked a group that needed a greater challenge to "hit a moving target."

A health education teacher presented the following to her students:

Group 1. As a sports nutritionist, create a menu plan for a week for a female athlete who weighs 130 pounds and is 5' 5" tall and plays on a soccer team.

Group 2. As a diet expert, create a menu plan for a week for a 15-year-old boy who wants to build muscle and put on weight before football season.

Group 3. During the next week, write down everything you eat and calculate the nutritional value as well as the caloric value. Use the computer program to help you.

She felt that these three groups of students would be challenged by these problems, so she provided a variety of contexts that would suit each one. The third group of students were allowed the limited computer access available in the classroom because they needed that support to manage the calculations. The teacher's focus was on nutritional understanding and analysis, and she felt that the mathematical calculations would frustrate them and slow them down, thus losing their interest. Students were asked about their preferences before this assignment.

Posing problems with open-ended solutions is a great way to meet the learners where they are and engage them in accessing information and coming up with creative solutions. Problems are useful at any grade level and with almost any subject matter. They are adjustable for different levels of readiness, complexity, and abstractness. As with projects, the students seek their levels of comfort and creativity and choose the "size that fits."

Inquiry, research, or independent study is another curricular model that engages students at their levels and interests. The inquiry model in Figure 61 is a simple flow chart that helps teachers take students through the process, beginning with an exploratory phase to define the topic, and build background experiences and knowledge. The next step is selecting a focus and posing a question that they wish to explore. They examine alternatives, consider and select the most appropriate one given their findings, and decide how to communicate their learning.

Figure 61.   Flow Chart for a Basic Inquiry Model

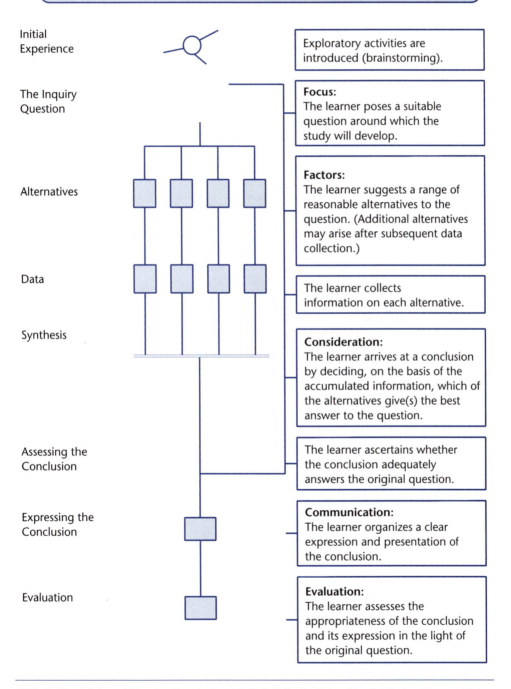

A BASIC INQUIRY MODEL

Initial Experience — Exploratory activities are introduced (brainstorming).

The Inquiry Question — **Focus:** The learner poses a suitable question around which the study will develop.

Alternatives — **Factors:** The learner suggests a range of reasonable alternatives to the question. (Additional alternatives may arise after subsequent data collection.)

Data — The learner collects information on each alternative.

Synthesis — **Consideration:** The learner arrives at a conclusion by deciding, on the basis of the accumulated information, which of the alternatives give(s) the best answer to the question.

Assessing the Conclusion — The learner ascertains whether the conclusion adequately answers the original question.

Expressing the Conclusion — **Communication:** The learner organizes a clear expression and presentation of the conclusion.

Evaluation — **Evaluation:** The learner assesses the appropriateness of the conclusion and its expression in the light of the original question.

SOURCE: From Ministry of Education, Ontario, *Research Study Skills: Curriculum Ideas for Teachers* (Toronto: Ministry of Education, 1979, p. 20).

ACADEMIC CONTRACTS

Contracts (Berte, 1975; Knowles, 1986; Robbins, Gregory, & Herndon, 2000; Tomlinson, 1998, 1999; Winebrenner, 1992) have often been used to allow students some flexibility and choice in their learning. Contracts have the potential for students to develop "flow," the state in which they are totally engaged in a challenging and motivating task that matches their skills and preferences.

Academic contracts allow learners to

- Be clear about expectations
- Use their multiple intelligences
- Take ownership of their learning
- Learn to manage time and task

When teachers set up an academic contract, they consider the standards that will be targeted and the objectives in the subject content that will be embedded in the choices. Assessment tools, timelines, and clear expectations should be identified up front.

The example in Figure 62 offers students eight choices for a culminating activity for a unit on World War II, plus a wild card for students to design an optional activity to be finished during the unit at their own pace. To use contracts, some class time would be given for conferencing with the teacher about choices and to gather resources. Students could also work on this project as a sponge activity whenever regular class work was completed. After students select one of the options, they fill in the contract form (see Figure 63).

Some teachers use a double-duty log (see Figure 26 in Chapter 5) so students can keep track of time, process, and progress.

Another type of contract is one in which the teacher provides some core activities that all students will complete plus several options from which individual students can choose. An example is shown in Figure 64.

Figure 62. Choice Board for Study of World War II

1	2	3
Design four posters using your own drawings or pictures that depict the characteristics of life during World War II. Use captions to explain your visuals.	Develop an interview questionnaire; then interview at least four people who lived in this area during World War II. Describe at last five ways the war affected their lives.	Write and present a short one-act play that depicts life during World War II, either at home or overseas. Use support material from novels or historical references.
4	**5**	**6**
Read a book, such as *The Diary of Anne Frank,* and briefly describe four scenarios from the story showing how World War II changed the characters' lives.	Wild Card! Your choice. Please design an option and present it in writing by_____.	Produce a PowerPoint presentation using visuals, scripts, and sound to present life as one would have experienced it during World War II.
7	**8**	**9**
Listen to a variety of songs, musicals, and film soundtracks composed during World War II. Referring to the content of the songs, describe what the music conveys about what life was like during the war.	Collect a variety of pictures, newspaper articles, photographs, poems, and stories. Noting aspects of life during World War II, create a personal diary of how you would have felt growing up in that time.	Create a board game designed to increase understanding of what life was like during World War II.

Teacher Direction: Put a choice in each box. Use as many boxes as needed. There should be more lines on the total choice board than there are students in the classroom. This gives the last group a chance to have a selection.

Student Direction: Sign up for the one you choose.

Figure 63.   Contract Form for Student to Fill In After Choosing an Activity

Name _____ Unit of Study _____

I agree to complete the following activity: _____

_____

I chose this option because _____

_____

_____

Please outline your plan: _____

_____

_____

_____

_____

_____

_____

_____

_____

_____

_____

_____

By the (date) _____

Signature _____

Figure 64. Contract Form In Which the Teacher Provides Some Core Activities

Author Study Contract

To help you improve your reading and writing, you will complete the core activities and may choose any optional activities that total at least 40 points.

Please fill in the contract and hand it in by _____.

Core Activities That Everyone Will Do: (Points)

1. I will select and begin a book by _____. (5)

2. I will create a "mind map" character sketch about a main character in my book, (appearance, personality, friends/family, likes/dislikes). (10)

3. Each author uses language in interesting ways. Select 3 passages that you think are unique and explain in your own words their meaning and why you think the author expressed himself or herself in this way. (10)

Optional Selections:

4. I will write a dialogue that I could role-play about a situation or problem that I read (1 page). (10)

5. I will draw a story map or comic strip with captions outlining the plot. (10)

6. I will write a commercial, design a poster, or produce a brochure on the computer to advertise my book and/or the author. (5)

7. As a critic, I will write an article sharing my thoughts about the story, outlining what I thought was Plus, Minus, and Interesting (de Bono, 1987). This will be a full-page column. I will use the word-processing program on the computer. (10)

8. Design an option and discuss with the teacher. (5 or 10)

This will give me _____ points.

Signed by Student _____

Signed by Teacher _____

Sample Units That Use Contracts

Sample Unit 1: What Makes a Community?[1]

Introduction: Over the next few weeks, we will be studying communities. You will be involved in many different activities that will help you understand why learning communities are established and how different people help keep a learning community working. Some of the activities will be completed by everyone in the class. You will be able to select other things to be completed on your own or with a group of your classmates.

Evaluation criteria:

- Thorough in-depth research.
- All information is relevant.
- You stayed on task without reminders.
- Neatness.
- Originality.
- Working with others and helping your group.
- Careful use of computer equipment.

Directions: Read the list of activities below. When you decide on the activities you would like to complete on your own or with a group, please fill out the form, sign, and turn in the community "Learning Contract Agreement" at the end of this assignment.

Everyone in class will complete the following activities:

Done	Activity	Number of Points
	Using Inspiration software, create a mind map (concept map, many pictures) of your community.	10
	Find a problem in the community. How would you solve this problem?	5
	Make a book about "Where Do People Live?" Draw pictures and describe the different places you draw.	10
	Design a community model. Include the things you have learned about, such as libraries, banks, park buildings, museums, schools, hospitals, and police stations.	35
	Conduct an Internet search to find out about other communities and their workers. Listen to or read stories about their jobs.	10

1. SOURCE: Used with permission from Sarward Baig and Linda Smeutek (Hayt Elementary, Chicago).

Select from these optional activities so that your total project points will be at least 100 points.

Done	Activity	Points
	1. Create a travel brochure about your community. Your brochure should make people outside of your community want to come visit your community. How will you make your community seem special? What are some of the best things you can say about your community? Be sure to use pictures and words to make your brochure attractive and professional looking.	15
	2. Survey people (at least 10) in your community to find out their favorite places in their community. You might ask the following questions: (a) What is your favorite restaurant? (b) What is your favorite building? or (c) Who is your favorite veterinarian? First, decide how you will find out the information. Will you ask people yourself, or will you create a written survey to give them? How will you keep track of their responses? Finally, make a poster that shows your survey results. Show the favorite places in the community.	10
	3. What makes our community special? Draw pictures of people helping others, important community centers and places, and community events.	10
	4. Create a slideshow that clearly explains what a community is. The show should include the different types of community, community service workers, cultures, customs, and government. Include graphics (pictures, cartoons, maps, etc.).	15
	5. Complete a puzzle that shows a job within the community.	5
	6. What do you want to be? Draw a picture of the community helper you would like to be. Draw pictures of the helper's workplace and equipment.	10
	7. Design a building for a community and write about why it is an important building for a community. Be sure to answer these questions: What is the name of the building? What makes it unique? How does it meet the needs of the people living in the community? What roles will people who work in the building play in the community?	10
	8. Use a computer program to draw a community map. Make sure to include a map key and cardinal directions.	10

What Makes a Community Contract? I, _____ agree to work on these activities to bring my total community unit points to at least 100 points. Here is a list of the extra activities I have chosen.

Extra Activities #1 and #2 Need Teacher Input	*Points*
1.	
2.	
3.	
4.	
5.	

I understand that my work will be evaluated based on the following criteria:

- Thorough in-depth research.
- All information is relevant.
- I stayed on task without reminders.
- Neatness.
- Working with others and helping the group finish a project.
- Careful use of computer equipment.

I understand that my contract work must be turned in by _____.

I will work on the contract activities that I select during class time unless I first discuss with my teacher doing something outside of class.

I agree to stay on task while working on my contract activities so that I do not distract others and so that I can put forth my best effort.

Student's Signature _____ Date _____

Teacher's Signature _____ Date _____

Sample Unit 2: Reading Workshop Contract[2]

Week of_____

I agree to make just the right book selections and READ and READ so I can . . .

Assignment	Done!
Write a letter to _____	
Write a book recommendation	
Answer the question: Who is the trickiest villain: the big bad pig, Coyote, or the shark? Why? (Use support from the book to answer your question!)	

I will choose one from the following! Check off your choice.

• Compare and contrast the Three Little Javelinas and the Three Hawaiian Pigs using a Venn diagram.	
• Make up riddles for your vocabulary words. Have a partner try to figure them out!	
• Collect shark facts and share them with the class.	
• Write a letter to the shark giving him advice on a new disguise. Draw a picture of it.	
• Write a paragraph describing a house that you would build if you were one of the pigs from the story. Answer the questions: What would it be made of? What would it look like? Where would it be? Draw a picture!	

I understand that I also need to continue my reading!
I agree to try my very best to complete all of my work. I will pay attention to directions and ask questions if things are unclear.

Signature _____ **Date** _____

---

2. SOURCE: Adapted from an idea from Ana Solis at Mayer Elementary, in Chicago.

Teachers need to ask certain questions as they plan and design a contract. Use the questions in Figure 65 to help plan contracts.

All these curriculum approaches allow for adjustments in the learning, offer variety guided by the standards, and engage the learners with intriguing and thoughtful learning activities.

Figure 65.   Questions Teachers Need to Ask Themselves
as They Plan and Design Contracts

What are the standards, content, and skills that will be embedded in this contract? _____

_____

How long will the contract last? _____

What types of activities will support the standards and interest diverse learners? _____

_____

Brainstorm possibilities! _____

_____

What are the core activities that everyone will participate in? _____

_____

Should I design more than one contract considering the readiness of my students by examining the pre-assessment (simple-to-complex, concrete-to-abstract thinking)? _____

What weight should each task be assigned (points)? _____

PUTTING IT ALL TOGETHER IN YOUR DIFFERENTIATED CLASSROOM

8

IN OUR QUEST TO FIND THE BEST FIT FOR OUR STUDENTS, WE NEED to recognize that change is a process, not an event (Fullan, 1991), and that we are on a journey of continuous improvement.

Day-to-day planning takes time, especially when our planning involves the process of rethinking what we have done in the past in the one-size-fits-all classroom. We still "begin with the end in mind," focusing on the standards and expectations in the curriculum, but now we also adjust and redesign the learning activities, tailoring them to the needs and preferences of the unique learners in each classroom. We also need to consider how the brain operates, and we should always strive to use research-based best practices when planning instruction, to ensure that we are being effective in our efforts to maximize student learning.

Throughout this book, we have suggested many ideas and strategies to fill your tool kits. Coming full circle in this chapter, we will revisit the lesson-planning template from Chapter 1 and the adjustable-assignments grid from Chapter 5. We will apply the template (see Figure 66, page 172) and the grid (Figure 67, page 173) to a variety of differentiated lessons at various levels—early, elementary, middle, and high school—and we will also use them to differentiate by content, interest, readiness, and multiple intelligences for the diverse learners in our classrooms: those just beginning, those approaching content mastery, and those already at a high degree of content mastery (see Figures 67–73, pages 173–179). Differentiation does *not* mean always tiering every lesson for three levels of complexity or challenge. It does mean finding interesting, engaging, and appropriate ways of honoring diversity and helping students learn new concepts and skills.

We think it is important to start small but to think big, too. If you aim for just 1 new "gourmet" lesson each week, you'll have 40 at the end of the year.

Teachers and schools should have a moral purpose, they say. But "they" usually present too few ideas about what that moral purpose should be. Not just any purpose will do. Schools should reach for higher educational purposes that truly are moral in transforming children's lives and building a better world for the generations of the future. Among the many purposes of schooling, four stand out to us as having special moral value: to love and care, to serve, to empower, and, of course, to learn (Hargreaves & Fullan, 1998). Educators need to celebrate how dedicated they are to meeting the needs of their students and how strategic teaching and learning have become.

The chart in Figure 74 (page 180) offers questions for reflection by teachers as they move toward differentiated learning for their students.

Figure 66.   The Six-Step Planning Model for Differentiated Learning: Template

Planning for Differentiated Learning

1. STANDARDS: What should students know and be able to do?	Assessment tools for data collection: (logs, checklists, journals, agendas, observations, portfolios, rubrics, contracts)
Essential Questions:	

2. CONTENT: (concepts, vocabulary, facts)	**SKILLS:**

3. ACTIVATE: Focus Activity: Pre-assessment strategy Pre-assessment Prior knowledge & engaging the learners	• Quiz, test • Surveys • K-W-L • Journals • Arm gauge • Give me • Brainstorm • Concept formation • Thumb it
4. ACQUIRE: Total group or small groups	• Lecturette • Presentation • Demonstration • Jigsaw • Video • Field trip • Guest speaker • Text
5. Grouping Decisions: (TAPS, random, heterogeneous, homogeneous, interest, task, constructed) **APPLY** **ADJUST**	• Learning centers • Projects • Contracts • Compact/Enrichment • Problem based • Inquiry • Research • Independent study
6. ASSESS Diversity Honored (learning styles, multiple intelligences, personal interest, etc.)	• Quiz, test • Performance • Products • Presentation • Demonstration • Log, journal • Checklist • Portfolio • Rubric • Metacognition

Figure 67.   Adjustable-Assignments Grid to Record Data
About Student Readiness Levels: Template

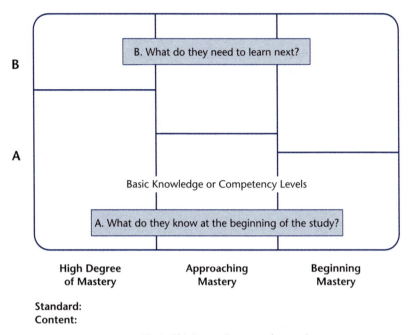

B. What do they need to learn next?

B

A

Basic Knowledge or Competency Levels

A. What do they know at the beginning of the study?

| High Degree | Approaching | Beginning |
| of Mastery | Mastery | Mastery |

Standard:
Content:

Note: This is not about number or time

Figure 68. Planning for Differentiated Learning for Early Elementary Math: Reading the Analog Clock/Telling Time

Planning for Differentiated Learning

1. STANDARDS: What should students know and be able to do? Read the clock to the minute. Count time using minutes. Count time using minutes and seconds. Learn how to read the clock for all times.	Assessment tools for data collection: (logs, checklists, journals, agendas, observations, portfolios, rubrics, contracts)
Essential Questions: What time is it?	

2. CONTENT: (concepts, vocabulary, facts) digital clock, hours, minutes, seconds, AM, PM	**SKILLS:** Reading the clock accurately in the same hour on most occasions. Reading the time on the digital clock when given a specific time and show it on the digital clock. Understanding a clock and how it works.

3. ACTIVATE:　　　Focus Activity:　　　Pre-assessment strategy Pre-assessment Prior knowledge & engaging the learners Label the minute and hour hands, seconds. Describe ½, ¼, and on the hour time. Name and discuss five important times in your daily schedule.	• Quiz, test • Surveys • K-W-L • Journals • Arm gauge • Give me • Brainstorm • Concept formation • Thumb it

4. ACQUIRE: Total group or small groups Use individual manipulative clocks to show various times. Partners explain how the hour and minute hands work. In a small group, have students brainstorm about when they would need a digital clock so they are aware of the value of learning the skill. Small groups race to find the assigned accurate time on their manipulative clocks.	• Lecturette • Presentation • Demonstration • Jigsaw • Video • Field trip • Guest speaker • Text

5. Grouping Decisions: (TAPS, random, heterogeneous, homogeneous, interest, task, constructed) **APPLY** **ADJUST** **Beginning Mastery** Count by 5s with minute hand. Learn location of each hand: 　　on the hour 　　quarter past, 15 minutes 　　half hour, 30 minutes 　　quarter 'til, 45 minutes **Approaching Mastery** Read the clock to the minute. Count time using minutes. Count time using minutes and seconds. Learn how to read the clock for all times. **High Degree of Mastery** Needs opportunities to read the clock for all times automatically.	• Learning centers • Projects • Contracts • Compact/Enrichment • Problem based • Inquiry • Research • Independent study

6. ASSESS Students will show the right time on the clock faces when given a specific time. Test on the parts of the clock. Diversity Honored (learning styles, multiple intelligences, personal interest, etc.)	• Quiz, test • Performance • Products • Presentation • Demonstration • Log, journal • Checklist • Portfolio • Rubric • Metacognition

Figure 69. Adjustable-Assignments Grid for Early Elementary Math:
Understanding the Clock and Elapsed Time

Standard, Concept, or Skill: Elapsed Time
Level: Upper Elementary
Key

A. What the learners know at the beginning of the study.
B. What the learners need to learn next.

B Needs to read the clock for all times automatically.	Read the clock to the minute. Count time using minutes. Count time using minutes and seconds. Learn how to read the clock for all times.	Count by 5s with minute hand. The hour hand moves more slowly than the minute hand. Learn location: ___ O'clock: On the hour and location of each hand: quarter past, 5 minutes, half hour, 30 minutes, quarter 'til, 45 minutes.
A Uses the clock daily. Explains how the hour and minute hands work. Reads the clock accurately in the same hour on most occasions.	Tells time accurately on hour and half hour. Recognizes time on clock of routines such as lunch time or dismissal time. Understands and reads accurately elapsed time on the hour.	Reads a digital clock. Can name parts of the clock: minute hand, hour hand Knows 60 minutes is an hour. Knows 12 numbers represent hours.
High Degree of Mastery	**Approaching Mastery**	**Beginning Mastery**

Figure 70. Planning for Differentiated Learning for Upper Elementary Science: Interpreting the Periodic Table

Planning for Differentiated Learning

1. STANDARDS: What should students know and be able to do? Read and interpret the periodic table. Interpret charted data. Learn each element and its location on the periodic table.	Assessment tools for data collection: (logs, checklists, journals, agendas, observations, portfolios, rubrics, contracts)

Essential Questions:
What does each element represent on the periodic table?
What are the elements, and what do they mean?

2. CONTENT: (concepts, vocabulary, facts) Element names and attributes of periodic table	**SKILLS:** Interpreting data and terminology. Learning how to read the periodic table. Learning how the periodic table is designed and its purpose. Needs a thorough explanation of the process of working with the periodic table.

3. ACTIVATE: Focus Activity: Pre-assessment strategy Pre-assessment Prior knowledge & engaging the learners Can use a given key on the table. Locates and changes substance particles. Recognizes the periodic table. Learn the terminology. Use the key on the table. Learn the common elements and characteristics.	• Quiz, test • Surveys • K-W-L • Journals • Arm gauge • Give me • Brainstorm • Concept formation • Thumb it

4. ACQUIRE: Total group or small groups Interpret the data on the entries on the table. Determine number and mass by using the table accurately. Name reasons behind columns and rows. Name basic formulas using the table.	• Lecturette • Presentation • Demonstration • Jigsaw • Video • Field trip • Guest speaker • Text

5. Grouping Decisions: (TAPS, random, heterogeneous, homogeneous, interest, task, constructed) **APPLY** **ADJUST** **Beginning Mastery** Recognize the periodic table. Learn the terminology. Use the key on the table. Learn the common elements and characteristics. **Approaching Mastery** Learn how the periodic table is developed. Needs a thorough explanation of the process of working the periodic table. **High Degree of Mastery** Apply combinations of elements. Use the table with real-world problems and situations.	• Learning centers • Projects • Contracts • Compact/Enrichment • Problem based • Inquiry • Research • Independent study

6. ASSESS The definition and process of using the periodic table. Interpreting the table key. What does each entry stand for and mean? How does the table work? Who uses the periodic table, and when? Diversity Honored (learning styles, multiple intelligences, personal interest, etc.)	• Quiz, test • Performance • Products • Presentation • Demonstration • Log, journal • Checklist • Portfolio • Rubric • Metacognition

| **Figure 71.** | Adjustable-Assignments Grid for Upper Elementary Science: Interpreting the Periodic Table |

Standard, Concept, or Skill: Interpreting the Periodic Table

Key

A. List specific knowledge base that the students know at the beginning of the study. This has been determined by a well-planned pre-assessment.

B. To determine B, the teacher lists what each group of learners need to learn next. This challenges those who have a strong background at the high degree of mastery level, determines what those learners who are ready for the information need, and determines the gaps of those who do not have the basic knowledge needed to learn the information being taught.

B	Apply combinations of elements. Use the table with real-world problems and situations.	Learn how the periodic table is developed. Needs a thorough explanation of the process of working with the periodic table.	Recognize the periodic table. Learn the terminology. Use the key on the table. Learn the common elements and characteristics.
A	Determines number and mass by using the table accurately. Understands reasons behind columns and rows. Is able to write basic formulas using the table.	Understands the terminology. Can use a given key on the table. Locates and changes substance particles.	Knows a few common elements. Has heard the term *periodic table*.

| **High Degree of Mastery** | **Approaching Mastery** | **Beginning Mastery** |

Figure 72. Planning for Differentiated Learning for Middle School Science: Exploring the Functions of the Body's Skeletal and Muscular Systems

Planning for Differentiated Learning

1. STANDARDS: What should students know and be able to do? Skeletal and muscular systems work together to carry out the life function of locomotion.	Assessment tools for data collection: (logs, checklists, journals, agendas, observations, portfolios, rubrics, contracts)

Essential Questions:
What functions do skeletal and muscular systems provide? How do we better care for these systems?

2. CONTENT: (concepts, vocabulary, facts) Muscles, skeleton, functions, ligaments, bones	**SKILLS:** Visual representations Cause and effect

3. ACTIVATE: Pre-assessment Prior knowledge & engaging the learners	Focus Activity: Pre-assessment strategy 3 Functions of skeletal/muscular system 2 Questions you would like to ask 1 Reason why this is good to know Label the parts of the skeletal & muscular systems	• Quiz, test • Surveys • K-W-L • Journals • Arm gauge • Give me • Brainstorm • Concept formation • Thumb it
4. ACQUIRE: Total group or small groups View video in groups of 3 with an advanced organizer. Small group discussion and fill in advance organizer as a summarizing and note-taking piece. Compare information from video with textbook reading working with a random partner.		• Lecturette • Presentation • Demonstration • Jigsaw • Video • Field trip • Guest speaker • Text

5. Grouping Decisions: (TAPS, random, heterogeneous, homogeneous, interest, task, constructed)			• Learning centers • Projects
APPLY **ADJUST**	Students will group according to the choices they make from the choice board	Students will work alone, in pairs or trios to complete two projects on the choice board.	Students will present their projects from the choice board. Teacher and peers provide feedback with rubric.	• Contracts • Compact/Enrichment • Problem based • Inquiry • Research • Independent study

6. ASSESS Students will individually write a paper on the necessity and functions of the skeletal and muscular systems and their efforts to take care of these systems for healthy living. Test on parts and functions of the two systems. Diversity Honored (learning styles, multiple intelligences, personal interest, etc.)	• Quiz, test • Performance • Products • Presentation • Demonstration • Log, journal • Checklist • Portfolio • Rubric • Metacognition

In this lesson, the strategies for learning are being differentiated. The teacher does a quick informative pre-assessment to find out what the students know. Their interest is stimulated with a variety of audio, visual, and print materials and ongoing discussion in cooperative small groups. Choice is provided with a Tic-Tac-Toe or Choice Board so that students can rehearse content and present their understandings in a variety of ways.

Differentiation is not always three levels of complexity or challenge, but interesting, engaging, and appropriate ways of learning new concepts and skills.

Figure 73. Planning for Differentiated Learning for High School Social Studies: Examining the Impact of European Immigration on American Culture

Planning for Differentiated Learning

1. STANDARDS: What should students know and be able to do? Examine the influx of European immigrants and their contributions to American society.	Assessment tools for data collection: (logs, checklists, journals, agendas, observations, portfolios, rubrics, contracts)

Essential Questions:
How has the ethnicity of immigrants in the early 21st century influenced and affected our lives in the United States?

2. CONTENT: (concepts, vocabulary, facts) Immigration, culture, emigration, relocation, ethnicity, employment, religion	**SKILLS:** Compare and contrast. Research and data collection. Visual representation.

3. ACTIVATE: Focus Activity: Pre-assessment strategy Pre-assessment Prior knowledge & engaging the learners Students create a four-corner organizer to fill in what they know about immigration at the beginning of the 21st century. Each student will generate a personal question. Guest speaker: immigrant grandparent.	• Quiz, test • Surveys • K-W-L • Journals • Arm gauge • Give me • Brainstorm • Concept formation • Thumb it
4. ACQUIRE: Total group or small groups From an interest survey, students identify which groups of immigrants they would like to investigate more thoroughly. Students will use the Internet, text, resource center, and community resources to gather information on a W5 chart.	• Lecturette • Presentation • Demonstration • Jigsaw • Video • Field trip • Guest speaker • Text
5. Grouping Decisions: (TAPS, random, heterogeneous, homogeneous, interest, task, constructed) **APPLY** **ADJUST** Students in small groups will present their findings to the total class. Each student will partner with another student who investigated a different ethnicity of immigrants using a cross-classification matrix. Students will regroup until the entire chart is filled in and all students have discussed all immigrant groups.	• Learning centers • Projects • Contracts • Compact/Enrichment • Problem based • Inquiry • Research • Independent study
6. ASSESS Students will create a "mindmap" in small groups to symbolize the contributions of immigrants to the American culture. Test on immigration in the early 21st century and the impact of the different ethnic groups. Diversity Honored (learning styles, multiple intelligences, personal interest, etc.)	• Quiz, test • Performance • Products • Presentation • Demonstration • Log, journal • Checklist • Portfolio • Rubric • Metacognition

This lesson focuses on best practices of note taking and summarizing using the four-corner organizer, so students can record the information about immigrant groups as a pre-assessment activity. Generating personal questions commits students to further investigation of the topic. Using an interest survey also helps students connect to the content in a personal way.

There are a variety of resources to facilitate investigation of immigrant groups. TAPS is used throughout the learning experience. The total group completes an interest survey. Learners identify personal interests independently. Students work in pairs and small groups at various different times. Students have multiple rehearsals using a variety of instructional strategies. Learning styles are respected: auditory, visual, tactile/kinesthetic.

Figure 74.   Checklist of Questions for Teachers Planning
Differentiated Learning for Their Students

B uilding Safe Environments

- Do students feel safe to risk and experiment with ideas?
- Do students feel included in the class and supported by others?
- Are tasks challenging enough without undo or "dis" stress?
- Is there an emotional "hook" for the learners?
- Are there novel, unique, and engaging activities to capture and sustain attention?
- Are "unique brains" honored and provided for? (learning styles & multiple intelligences)

R ecognizing and Honoring Diversity

- Does the learning experience appeal to the learners' varied and multiple intelligences and learning styles?
- May the students work collaboratively and independently?
- May they "show what they know" in a variety of ways?
- Does the cultural background of the learners influence instruction?

A ssessment

- Are pre-assessments given to determine readiness?
- Is there enough time to explore, understand, and transfer the learning to long-term memory (grow dendrites)? Is there time to accomplish mastery?
- Do they have opportunities for ongoing, "just in time" feedback?
- Do they have time to revisit ideas and concepts to connect or extend them?
- Is metacognitive time built into the learning process?
- Do students use logs and journals for reflection and goal setting?

I nstructional Strategies

- Are the expectations clearly stated and understood by the learner?
- Will the learning be relevant and useful to the learner?
- Does the learning build on past experience or create a new experience?
- Does the learning relate to their real world?
- Are strategies developmentally appropriate and hands on?
- Are the strategies varied to engage and sustain attention?
- Are there opportunities for projects, creativity, problems, and challenges?

N umerous Curriculum Approaches

- Do students work alone, in pairs, and in small groups?
- Do students work in learning centers based on interest, need, or choice?
- Are some activities adjusted to provide appropriate levels of challenge?
- Is pretesting used to allow for compacting/enrichment?
- Are problems, inquires, and contracts considered?

BIBLIOGRAPHY

Aronson, E. (1978). *The jigsaw classroom.* Beverly Hills, CA: Sage.

Bellanca, J., & Fogarty, R. (1991). *Blueprints for thinking in the cooperative classroom.* Thousand Oaks, CA: Corwin Press.

Bennett, B., Rolheiser-Bennett, C., & Stevahn, L. (1991). *Cooperative learning: Where heart meets mind.* Toronto, Canada: Educational Connections.

Berte, N. (1975). *Individualizing education by learning contracts.* San Francisco: Jossey-Bass.

Black, P., Harrison, C., Lee, C., Marshall, B., & Wiliam, D. (2004). Working inside the black box: Assessment for learning in the classroom. *Phi Delta Kappan, 86*(1), 8–21.

Bloom, B. S., et al. (1956). *Taxonomy of educational objectives. Handbook 1: Cognitive domain.* New York: David McKay.

Brooks, J., & Brooks, M. (1993). *In search of understanding: The case for constructivist classrooms.* Alexandria, VA: Association for Supervision and Curriculum Development.

Burke, K. (1993). *The mindful school: How to assess authentic learning.* Thousand Oaks, CA: Corwin Press.

Burke, K., Fogarty, R., & Belgrad, S. (1994). *The portfolio connection.* Thousand Oaks, CA: Corwin Press.

Caine, G., Caine, R. N., & Crowell, S. (1994). *Mindshifts: A brain-based process for restructuring schools and renewing education.* Tucson, AZ: Zephyr.

Caine, R. N., & Caine, G. (1991). *Making connections: Teaching and the human brain.* Alexandria, VA: Association for Supervision and Curriculum Development.

Caine, R. N., & Caine, G. (1994). *Making connections: Teaching and the human brain.* Reading, MA: Addison-Wesley.

Caine, R. N., & Caine, G. (1997). *Education on the edge of possibility.* Alexandria, VA: Association for Supervision and Curriculum Development.

Campbell, D. (1998). *The Mozart effect.* New York: Avon.

Cantelon, T. (1991a). *The first 4 weeks of cooperative learning, activities, and materials.* Portland, OR: Prestige.

Cantelon, T. (1991b). *Structuring the classroom successfully for cooperative team learning.* Portland, OR: Prestige.

Cardoso, S. H. (2000). Our ancient laughing brain. *Cerebrum: The Dana Forum on Brain Science, 2*(4), 15–30.

Chapman, C. (1993). *If the shoe fits: How to develop multiple intelligences in the classroom.* Thousand Oaks, CA: Corwin Press.

Chapman, C., & Freeman, L. (1996). *Multiple intelligences centers and projects.* Thousand Oaks, CA: Corwin Press.

Chapman, C., & King, R. (2000). *Test success in the brain-compatible classroom.* Tucson, AZ: Zephyr Press.

Chapman, C., & King, R. (2003a). *Differentiated instructional strategies for reading in the content areas.* Thousand Oaks, CA: Corwin Press.

Chapman, C., & King, R. (2003b). *Differentiated instructional strategies for writing in the content areas.* Thousand Oaks, CA: Corwin Press.

Chapman, C., & King, R. (2005). *Differentiated assessment strategies: One tool doesn't fit all.* Thousand Oaks, CA: Corwin Press.

Chapman, C., & King, R. (2007a). *Differentiated reading and writing strategies for elementary classrooms* (Multimedia kit). Thousand Oaks, CA: Corwin Press.

Chapman, C., & King, R. (2007b). *Differentiated reading and writing strategies for secondary classrooms* (Multimedia kit). Thousand Oaks, CA: Corwin Press.

Clarke, J., Wideman, R., & Eadie, S. (1990). *Together we learn.* Scarborough, Canada: Prentice Hall.

Costa, A. (1995). *Outsmarting I.Q.: The emerging science of learnable intelligence.* Old Tappan, NJ: Free Press.

Cowan, G., & Cowan, E. (1980). *Writing.* New York: John Wiley.

Csikszentmihalyi, M. (1990). *Flow: The psychology of optimal experience.* New York: HarperCollins.

Damasio, A. R. (1994). *Descartes' error.* New York: Putnam.

de Bono, E. (1987). *CoRT thinking program.* Elmsford, NY: Pergamon.

DePorter, B., Reardon, M., & Singer-Nourie, S. (1998). *Quantum teaching.* Boston: Allyn & Bacon.

Diamond, M., & Hopson, J. (1998). *Magic trees of the mind.* New York: Penguin.

Diamond, M. C. (1967). Extensive cortical depth measurements and neuron size increases in the cortex of environmentally enriched rats. *Journal of Comparative Neurology, 131,* 357–364.

Doyle, M., & Strauss, D. (1976). *How to make meetings work.* New York: Playboy.

Driscoll, M. E. (1994, April). *School community and teacher's work in urban settings: Identifying challenges to community in the school organization.* Paper presented at the annual meeting of the American Educational Research Association, New Orleans, LA. (Available from New York University)

Dunn, K., & Dunn, R. (1992). *Bringing out the giftedness in your child.* New York: John Wiley.

Dunn, R., & Dunn, K. (1987). Dispelling outmoded beliefs about student learning. *Educational Leadership, 44*(6), 55–61.

Ekwall, E. E., & Shanker, J. L. (1988). *Diagnosis and remediation of the disabled reader* (3rd ed.). Boston: Allyn & Bacon.

Fogarty, R. (1998). *Problem-based learning & other curricular models for the multiple intelligences classroom.* Thousand Oaks, CA: Corwin Press.

Fogarty, R., & Stoehr, J. (1995). *Integrating curricula with multiple intelligences: Teams, themes, and threads.* Thousand Oaks, CA: Corwin Press.

Fullan, M. (with Steigelbauer, S.). (1991). *The new meaning of educational change.* New York: Teachers College Press.

Gardner, H. (1983). *Frames of mind: The theory of multiple intelligences.* New York: Basic Books.

Gardner, H. (1993). *Multiple intelligences: The theory in practice.* New York: Basic Books.

Gibbs, J. (1995). *Tribes: A new way of learning and being together.* Santa Rosa, CA: Center Source.

Glasser, W. (1990). *The quality school.* New York: Harper & Row.

Glasser, W. (1998). *Choice theory in the classroom.* New York: HarperCollins.

Goleman, D. (1995). *Emotional intelligence.* New York: Bantam.

Goleman, D. (1998). *Working with emotional intelligence.* New York: Bantam.

Green, E. J., Greenough, W. T., & Schlumpf, B. E. (1983). Effects of complex or isolated environments on cortical dendrites of middle-aged rats. *Brain Research, 264,* 233–240.

Gregorc, A. (1982). *Inside styles: Beyond the basics.* Columbia, CT: Gregorc Associates.

Gregory, G. H. (2003). *Differentiated instructional strategies in practice.* Thousand Oaks, CA: Corwin Press.

Gregory, G. H. (2005). *Differentiating instruction with style.* Thousand Oaks, CA: Corwin Press.

Gregory, G. H., & Kuzmich, L. (2004). *Data-driven differentiation in the standards-based classroom.* Thousand Oaks, CA: Corwin Press.

Gregory, G. H., & Kuzmich, L. (2005a). *Differentiated literacy strategies for student growth and achievement in Grades K–6.* Thousand Oaks, CA: Corwin Press.

Gregory, G. H., & Kuzmich, L. (2005b). *Differentiated literacy strategies for student growth and achievement in Grades 7–12.* Thousand Oaks, CA: Corwin Press.

Gregory, G. H., & Kuzmich, L. (2007). *Teacher teams that get results: 61 group process skills and strategies.* Thousand Oaks, CA: Corwin Press.

Gregory, G. H., & Parry, T. S. (2006). *Designing brain-compatible learning* (3rd ed.). Thousand Oaks, CA: Corwin Press.

Hanson, J. R., & Silver, H. F. (1978). *Learning styles and strategies.* Moorestown, NJ: Hanson Silver Strong.

Hargreaves, S., & Fullan, M. (1998). *What's worth fighting for out there?* New York: Teachers College Press.

Harmin, M. (1994). *Inspiring active learning.* Alexandria, VA: Association for Supervision and Curriculum Development.

Hart, L. A. (1998). *Human brain and human learning.* Kent, WA: Books for Educators.

Healy, J. (1992). *Endangered minds: Why our children don't think.* New York: Simon & Schuster.

Hill, S., & Hancock. J. (1993). *Reading and writing communities.* Armadale, Australia: Eleanor Curtin.

Hunter, R. (2004). *Madeline Hunter's mastery teaching: Increasing instructional effectiveness in elementary and secondary schools* (Rev. ed.). Thousand Oaks, CA: Corwin Press.

Hyerle, D. (1996). *Visual tools for constructing knowledge.* Alexandria, VA: Association for Supervision and Curriculum Development.

Jensen, E. (1996). *Completing the puzzle: The brain-based approach.* Del Mar, CA: Turning Points.

Jensen, E. (1998a). *Introduction to brain-compatible learning.* Thousand Oaks, CA: Corwin Press.

Jensen, E. (1998b). *Teaching with the brain in mind.* Alexandria, VA: Association for Supervision and Curriculum Development.

Johnson, D. W., Johnson, R. T., & Holubec, E. J. (1998). *Cooperation in the classroom.* Edina, MN: Interaction Book.

Kagan, S. (1992). *Cooperative learning.* San Clemente, CA: Kagan Publishing.

Knowles, M. (1986). *Using learning contracts.* San Francisco: Jossey-Bass.

Kolb, D. (1984). *Experiential learning: Experience as the source of learning and development.* Englewood Cliffs, NJ: Prentice Hall.

Kotulak, R. (1996). *Inside the brain: Revolutionary discoveries of how the mind works.* Kansas City, MO: Andrews & McMeely.

LeDoux, J. (1996). *The emotional brain.* New York: Simon & Schuster.

Lou, Y., Alorami, P. C., Spence, J. C., Paulsen, C., Chambers, B., & d'Apollonio, S. (1996). Within-class grouping: A meta-analysis. *Review of Educational Research, 66*(4), 423–458.

Lyman, F., & McTighe, J. (1988, April). Cueing thinking in the classroom: The promise of theory-embedded tools. *Educational Leadership,* p. 7.

Marzano, R. J. (1992). *A different kind of classroom teaching with dimensions of learning.* Alexandria, VA: Association for Supervision and Curriculum Development.

Marzano, R. J., Pickering, D. J., & Pollack, J. E. (2001). *Classroom instruction that works.* Alexandria, VA: Association for Supervision and Curriculum Development.

Maslow, A. (1954). *Motivation and personality.* New York: Harper & Row.

Maslow, A. (1968). *Toward a psychology of being.* New York: Van Nostrand Reinhold.

McCarthy, B. (1990). Using the 4MAT system to bring learning styles to schools. *Educational Leadership, 48*(2), 31–37.

McCarthy, B., & McCarthy, D. (2006). *Teaching around the 4MAT cycle: Designing instruction for diverse learners with diverse learning styles.* Thousand Oaks, CA: Corwin Press.

McTighe, J. (1990). *Better thinking and learning* [Workshop handout]. Baltimore: Maryland State Department of Education.

Miller, G. (1956). The magical number seven, plus or minus two: Some limits on our capacity for processing information. *Psychological Review, 63,* 81–97.

Ogle, D. (1986). K-W-L: A teaching model that develops active reading of expository text. *Reading Teacher, 39,* 564–574.

O'Keefe, J., & Nadel, L. (1978). *The hippocampus as a cognitive map.* Oxford, UK: Clarendon.

Ornstein, R., & Thompson, R. (1984). *The amazing brain.* Boston: Houghton Mifflin.

Pascal-Leon, J. (1980). Compounds, confounds, and models in developmental information processing: A reply to Trabasso and Foellinger. *Journal of Experimental Child Psychology, 1,* 18–40.

Paulson, F. L., Paulson, P. R., & Meyer, C. A. (1991, February). What makes a portfolio a portfolio? *Educational Leadership,* pp. 60–63.

Pert, C. B. (1998). *Molecules of emotion.* New York: Scribner.

Peterson, L. R., & Peterson, M. J. (1959). Short-term retention of individual verbal items. *Journal of Experimental Psychology, 58,* 193–198.

Pinker, S. (1998). *How the mind works.* New York: Norton.

Reis, S., & Renzulli, J. (1992). Using curriculum compacting to challenge the above average. *Educational Leadership, 50*(2), 51–57.

Restak, R. (1993). *The brain has a mind of its own.* New York: Harmony.

Robbins, P., Gregory, G., & Herndon, L. (2000). *Thinking inside the block schedule.* Thousand Oaks, CA: Corwin Press.

Rolheiser, C., Bower, B., & Stevahn, L. (2000). *The portfolio organizer.* Alexandra, VA: Association for Supervision and Curriculum Development.

Rowe, M. B. (1988, Spring). Wait time: Slowing down may be a way of speeding up. *Educator,* p. 43.

Rozman, D. (1998, March). *Speech at Symposium on the Brain.* University of California, Berkeley.

Sapolsky, R. M. (1998). *Why zebras don't get ulcers.* New York: Freeman.

Silver, H., Strong, R., & Perini, M. (2000). *So each may learn: Integrating learning styles and multiple intelligences.* Alexandria, VA: Association for Supervision and Curriculum Development.

Slavin, R. E. (1994). *Cooperative learning: Theory, research, and practice.* Boston: Allyn & Bacon.

Smith, F. (1986). *Insult to intelligence.* New York: Arbor House.

Sousa, D. (1999). *Teaching manual for how the brain learns.* Thousand Oaks, CA: Corwin Press.

Sprenger, M. (1998). *Learning & memory: The brain in action.* Alexandria, VA: Association for Supervision and Curriculum Development.

Stepien, W., Gallagher, S., & Workman, D. (1993). Problem-based learning for traditional and interdisciplinary classrooms. *Journal for Gifted Education, 16,* 338–357.

Sternberg, R. (1996). *Successful intelligence: How practical and creative intelligence determine success in life.* New York: Simon & Schuster.

Stiggins, R. (1993). *Student-centered classroom assessment.* Englewood Cliffs, NJ: Prentice Hall.

Sylwester, R. (1995). *A celebration of neurons: An educator's guide to the brain.* Alexandria, VA: Association for Supervision and Curriculum Development.

Tomlinson, C. A. (1998). *Differentiating instruction: Facilitator's guide.* Alexandria, VA: Association for Supervision and Curriculum Development.

Tomlinson, C. A. (1999). *The differentiated classroom: Responding to the needs of all learners.* Alexandria, VA: Association for Supervision and Curriculum Development.

Tomlinson, C. A. (2001). *How to differentiate instruction in mixed-ability classrooms* (2nd ed.). Alexandria, VA: Association for Supervision and Curriculum Development.

Wiggins, G., & McTighe, J. (1998). *Understanding by design.* Alexandria, VA: Association for Supervision and Curriculum Development.

Winebrenner, S. (1992). *Teaching gifted kids in the regular classroom.* Minneapolis, MN: Free Spirit.

Wolfe, P. (2001). *Brain matters: Translating research into classroom practice.* Alexandria, VA: Association for Supervision and Curriculum Development.

Wolfe, P., & Sorgen, M. (1990). *Mind, memory and learning: Implications for the classroom.* Napa, CA: Author.

INDEX

CORWIN PRESS